WHATEVER IS TRUE

Return to Holistic Health

www.whateveristruehealth.com

Glen Aubrey

Creative Team Publishing
Fort Worth, Texas and San Diego, California

© **2022 by Glen Aubrey.**

All rights reserved. No part of this book may be reproduced, stored in a retrieval system or transmitted in any form or by any means without the prior written permission of the publisher, except by a reviewer who may quote brief passages in a review distributed through electronic media, or printed in a newspaper, magazine, or journal.

Disclaimers:

Due diligence has been exercised to obtain written permission for use of references, quotes, or imagery where required. Any additional quotes, references, or imagery may be subject to the Fair Use Doctrine. Where additional references, quotes, or imagery may require source credit, upon written certification that such a claim is accurate, credit for use will be noted on this website: **www.whateveristruehealth.com.**

- The opinions and conclusions expressed herein are solely those of the author and/or the individuals and entities represented. This work is unashamedly a book of religious faith in God, and reliance upon Him as Sovereign Lord, trusting His promises, and His truth.
- Views and opinions are quoted with permission, and are presented without regard to any political affiliation(s). Opinions and conclusions of contributors are limited to their telling of the facts, experiences, and circumstances involved.
- No professional, psychological, or medical advice is implied, stated, or offered in any way whatsoever. You are encouraged to seek professional help, education, advice,

and counsel from individuals you deem competent should you desire to learn more about the topics covered.
- Note: certain names and related circumstances may have been changed to protect confidentiality. All stories where names are mentioned are used with the permission of the parties involved, if applicable. Any resemblance to past or current people, places, circumstances, or events is purely coincidental.

Scripture:
- All Scripture references are quoted from the New International Version (NIV) of the Holy Bible, unless otherwise noted. **New International Version (NIV) Copyright © 1973, 1978, 1984, 2011 by Biblica, Inc ®** Used by permission. All rights reserved worldwide.

Website Design: Randy Beck www.mydomaintools.com
Cover design: Robin Johnson, RL Design
www.gobookcoverdesign.com

ISBN: 978-1-7350189-8-0

PUBLISHED BY CREATIVE TEAM PUBLISHING
www.CreativeTeamPublishing.com
Fort Worth, Texas and San Diego, California
Printed in the United States of America

Contents

Introduction:
    Philippians 4:8   9

    Philippians, Chapter 4   11

    Song: *It Is Well with My Soul*   20

Chapter One
    <u>True</u>
    Seeking What Is True — Timeless and Priceless
    By Everett (Bud) Hendrickson   25

Chapter Two
    <u>Noble</u>
    Politics and Media
    By John Culea   51

Chapter Three
    <u>Right</u>
    Fixed on Doing Right
    By Pastor James Patton   89

Contents

Chapter Four
    <u>Pure</u>
    Never Will God Leave You Comfortless
    By Glen Aubrey   129

Chapter Five
    <u>Lovely</u>
    The Eyes Have It
    By Glen Aubrey   147

Chapter Six
    <u>Admirable</u>
    By Glen Aubrey   159

Chapter Seven
    <u>Excellent</u>
    It's Time to Stand Up
    By Mickey Straub   167

Chapter Eight
    <u>Praiseworthy</u>
    Meditate on Praiseworthy
    By Jim Robeson   205

Chapter Nine
    <u>Think About Such Things</u>
    Values, Vision, Mission and Message,
    The Four Questions, The CORE TEAM, and
    A Value System
    By Glen Aubrey   223

Contents

Chapter Ten
    <u>Attributes, Attitudes, and Actions</u>
    By Glen Aubrey   *233*

    AAA Diagram   *235*

Chapter Eleven
    <u>Choices</u>
    By Glen Aubrey   *241*

    Song: *Gather The Children*, 1975   *260*

Chapter Twelve
    <u>Transformation, Change, and New Direction</u>
    By Rick Redd, MD   *267*

*****

Conclusion
    <u>Renewal: Return to Holistic Health</u>
    By Glen Aubrey   *291*

*****

Contents

Resources *297*

Appreciation *299*

The Author *301*

The Publisher and Printer *303*

*****

Philippians 4:8
(NIV)

Whatever is <u>true</u>,
    Whatever is <u>noble</u>,
        Whatever is <u>right</u>,
            Whatever is <u>pure</u>,
                Whatever is <u>lovely</u>,
                    Whatever is <u>admirable</u>,

If anything is <u>excellent</u>

        Or <u>praiseworthy</u>,

                <u>Think about such things</u>.

We are told what to think,
        And this admonition is for our good.

*****

Philippians, Chapter 4

Please notice the byline underneath the book's title. It is: "Return to Holistic Health."

Holistic Health is a phrase that encompasses far more than physical health, yet physical health is one manifestation of the meaning of 'holistic.'

Adapted from *Merriam-Webster*, © 2022: the term, "holistic" is built on holism: "a theory that the universe and especially living nature is correctly seen in terms of interacting wholes (as of living organisms) that are more than the mere sum of elementary particles; a study of method or treatment that is concerned with wholes or with complete systems : a holistic study or method of treatment."

We humans are complex and wonderful creations of God. In the Old Testament, David, as a young shepherd, then giant slayer (he leveled Goliath with a single stone from his sling shot), song writer (Psalmist), warrior, and eventual King of Israel, said this:

Philippians, Chapter 4

Psalm 139:14 (NIV)

I praise you because I am fearfully and
wonderfully made; your works are wonderful,
I know that full well.

David also committed many mistakes, or sins; and in spite of these he was called, "a man after God's own heart" before he sinned in the Old Testament and in a New Testament reference as well (I Samuel 13:14 and Acts 13:22). When confronted with his sin by Nathan, the prophet, David acknowledged his sin and repented. (2 Samuel 12)

I am convinced Almighty God designed us to be healthy and whole in multiple aspects of our earthly life experience; God created us to be holistic in body, mind, soul, and spirit. These aspects of us are connected and interwoven within each and every person.

> ... Almighty God designed us to be healthy and whole in multiple aspects of our earthly life experience;
> God created us to be holistic in body, mind, soul, and spirit. These aspects of us are connected and interwoven within each and every person.

I chose this subtitle, or byline, to indicate the complexity and marvelous creation that compose mankind. Involved in "holistic:" attitudes, attributes, and actions that compose what God's human creation is.

This book is written to persuade you that the attributes listed in Philippians 4:8 are interconnected pieces of life that show us what God desires of His people.

The Apostle Paul wrote the book of Philippians. His writing offers a higher motivation for living, a call for us to choose attitudes, attributes, and actions that attest to thought processes that are not commonly typical, and need to be. That is the purpose for Paul's instruction. He begins verse eight with, "Finally, brothers and sisters …"

It is interesting to note the context of this passage. Let's look, beginning with verse 4:

Philippians 4:4-9

Final Exhortations:

[4] Rejoice in the Lord always. I will say it again: Rejoice! [5] Let your gentleness be evident to all. The Lord is near.
[6] Do not be anxious about anything, but in every situation, by prayer and petition, with thanksgiving, present your requests to God.

⁷ And the peace of God, which transcends all understanding, will guard your hearts and your minds in Christ Jesus.
⁸ **Finally, brothers and sisters, <u>whatever is true, whatever is noble, whatever is right, whatever is pure, whatever is lovely, whatever is admirable — if anything is excellent or praiseworthy</u>** — think about such things.
⁹ Whatever you have learned or received or heard from me, or seen in me — put it into practice. And the God of peace will be with you.

*****

It may be helpful to get a dictionary definition of the words in Philippians 4:8. Here are the words and their definitions:

~ From **Merriam-Webster** 1828:

1. *True*: Conformable to fact; being in accordance with the actual state of things; as a true relation or narration; a true history. A declaration is true when it states the facts. In this sense, true is opposed to false.
2. *Noble*: Great; elevated; dignified; being above every thing that can dishonor reputation; as a noble mind; a *noble* courage; *noble* deeds of valor. Exalted; elevated; sublime.

Philippians, Chapter 4

3. ***Right***: just; equitable; accordant to the standard of truth and justice or the will of God. That alone is *right* in the sight of God, which is consonant to his will or law; this being the only perfect standard of truth and justice.
4. ***Pure***: Free from moral defilement; without spot; not sullied or tarnished; incorrupt; undebased by moral turpitude; holy.
5. ***Lovely***: Amiable; that may excite love; possessing qualities which may invite affection.
6. ***Admirable***: To be admired; worthy of admiration; having qualities to excite wonder, with approbation, esteem or reverence; used of persons or things; as, the *admirable* structure of the body, or of the universe.
7. ***Excellent***: Being of great virtue or worth; eminent or distinguished for what is amiable, valuable or laudable; as an excellent man or citizen; an excellent judge or magistrate; being of great value.
8. ***Praiseworthy:*** Deserving of praise or applause; commendable; as a praiseworthy action.

That is a meritorious list! According to this scripture, these traits of thought produce positive results, from exemplary actions.

How much of our thinking so often falls short of this standard, or is consumed by negativity, regardless of source?

Philippians, Chapter 4

A list of **direct opposites** may help us understand **how we are *not* to think**. Consider these words and traits in direct opposition to Paul's list.

The ***opposites*** (antonyms) of:

1. **True**: bad, dishonest, dishonorable, evil, immoral, indecent, sinful, unethical, unrighteous, wicked, wrong
2. **Noble**: baseborn, common, ignoble, low, mean
3. **Right**: improper, inapplicable, inappropriate, indecent, misbecoming, unbecoming, unfit, unseemly, unsuitable, wrong
4. **Pure**: coarse, dirty, filthy, immodest, indecent, obscene, smutty, unclean, vulgar
5. **Lovely**: grotesque, hideous, ill-favored, unattractive, unpleasing, unsightly
6. **Admirable**: censurable, discreditable, reprehensible
7. **Excellent**: atrocious, awful, lousy, pathetic, poor, rotten, terrible, vile, wretched
8. **Praiseworthy**: censurable, discreditable, reprehensible

How often do our thoughts become transfixed on the negative instead of the positive? When the opposites of the positive list become central to anyone's thinking, what kind of emotions do they produce? What are the results in life experience for you or anyone else? More to the point: is thinking like this healthy to body, mind, soul, and spirit?

Philippians, Chapter 4

The *results* of positive and uplifting thoughts are succinctly described by the Apostle Paul in verse nine of this same chapter: "… put into practice. <u>And the God of peace will be with you.</u>"

Think of it! What would we rather possess? Negative thoughts producing upsetting consequences including discord, or positive, Godly thoughts that usher in peace? This peace is not a surface emotion, though it can produce emotions that comfort the soul; it is far deeper. This peace is *at least* inward contentment, joy, gratitude, joyful longing, and satisfaction, giving life renewal to all who experience it.

In one verse before he begins this list, Paul describes this peace, stating it is "from God." His description is assuring to anyone who trusts in the goodness of the Almighty.

I invite you to read this verse slowly, out loud, pausing after every phrase.

Here is verse seven:

> "And the *peace* of God,
>   which *transcends all understanding,*
>   *will guard your hearts and your minds*
>   *in Christ Jesus.*"

This verse is worth unpacking further. First, the peace of God refers to tranquility and rest, and we are told that this peace is from God, that it rises "above human comprehension." This phraseology means, that you and I may not be able to appreciate it fully, because it is an experience in which we can share continually, without end. Further, it is applicable in *all* circumstances, including the positive and negative, even those which, on the surface, may be uncomfortable, unfavorable, and downright hard, disgusting, even demeaning.

The phrase, "guarding the heart," addresses protecting the core of every person. It is coupled with doing the same action for the mind. To "guard" anything means to defend, because we value what we are guarding. This guard and hedge of protection is another of the results of the indwelling and ruling of God's peace in our lives. We can only experience this kind of powerful, overcoming peace in a relationship with Christ Jesus as Lord, Master, Ruler, Redeemer, and Savior.

The sum total of God's peace is a transformed life, born of water (natural) and Spirit (supernatural). With God's peace in our hearts, we think, speak, and act differently in at least these areas:

1. Morally
2. Physically
3. Ethically
4. Politically

Philippians, Chapter 4

    5. Spiritually
    6. Soulfully

And in these arenas:
    7. Business
    8. Home, Family, and Extended Family
    9. Networks: Professionally, and Personally, including Neighbors
    10. When we meet New People, Strangers, and those who become Casual Acquaintances

And with these individuals:
    11. People who are Downtrodden and Less Fortunate
    12. People with whom we may not agree
    13. Leaders governmentally, whether we voted for them or not

And finally:
    14. With ***Everyone***

Please join me as we embark on this journey together.

Let's willfully choose a "holistic" approach to life, because this choice includes these attributes in Philippians and more: such as the Fruit or 'evidence' of the indwelling of the Spirit in our lives, recorded by Paul in the book of Galatians, Chapter 5, 22 – 23:

Philippians, Chapter 4

²² But the fruit of the Spirit is love, joy, peace, forbearance, kindness, goodness, faithfulness, ²³ gentleness and self-control. Against such things there is no law.

In the King James Version, there is a slight variation:

²² But the fruit of the Spirit is love, joy, peace, longsuffering, gentleness, goodness, faith, ²³ Meekness, temperance: against such there is no law.

The choices we make are preludes to our actions. Let's choose wisely.

> The choices we make are preludes to our actions. Let's choose wisely.

*****

One of my most revered and favorite old hymns of faith, written in the 19th century and first published in 1876, known and treasured the world over, is this one: ***It Is Well with My Soul.*** The melody was composed by Philip Paul Bliss, and lyrics were composed by Horatio G. Spafford.

According to Wikipedia:

Philippians, Chapter 4

This hymn was written after traumatic events in Spafford's life. The first two were the death of his four-year-old son and the Great Chicago Fire of 1871, which ruined him financially (he had been a successful lawyer and had invested significantly in property in the area of Chicago that was extensively damaged by the great fire).

His business interests were further hit by the economic downturn of 1873, at which time he had planned to travel to England with his family on the *SS Ville du Havre*, to help with Dwight L. Moody's upcoming evangelistic campaigns.

In a late change of plan, he sent the family ahead while he was delayed on business concerning zoning problems following the Great Chicago Fire. While crossing the Atlantic Ocean, the ship sank rapidly after a collision with a sea vessel, the *Loch Earn*, and all four of Spafford's daughters died. His wife Anna survived and sent him the now famous telegram, "Saved alone ..."

Shortly afterwards, as Spafford traveled to meet his grieving wife, he was inspired to write these words as his ship passed near where his daughters had died.

Philippians, Chapter 4

https://en.wikipedia.org/wiki/It_Is_Well_with_My_Soul - cite_note-loc-4 Bliss called his tune *Ville du Havre,* from the name of the stricken vessel.

~ McCann, Forrest Mason (1997). *Hymns & History: An Annotated Survey of Sources.* Abilene, Texas: ACU Press, pp. 327–328, 520, 597. ISBN 0-89112-058-0

Lyrics:

When peace like a river, attendeth my way,
When sorrows like sea billows roll;
Whatever my lot, Thou hast taught me to know
It is well, it is well, with my soul.

Refrain
It is well, (it is well),
With my soul, (with my soul)
It is well, it is well, with my soul.

Though Satan should buffet, though trials should come,
Let this blest assurance control,
That Christ has regarded my helpless estate,
And hath shed His own blood for my soul.

My sin, oh, the bliss of this glorious thought!
My sin, not in part but the whole,
Is nailed to the cross, and I bear it no more,
Praise the Lord, praise the Lord, O my soul!

Philippians, Chapter 4

For me, be it Christ, be it Christ hence to live:
If Jordan above me shall roll,
No pang shall be mine, for in death as in life,
Thou wilt whisper Thy peace to my soul.

But Lord, 'tis for Thee, for Thy coming we wait,
The sky, not the grave, is our goal;
Oh, trump of the angel! Oh, voice of the Lord!
Blessed hope, blessed rest of my soul.

And Lord, haste the day when the faith shall be sight,
The clouds be rolled back as a scroll;
The trump shall resound, and the Lord shall descend,
A song in the night, oh my soul!
~ This song is in the Public Domain.

We conclude this opening introduction by re-quoting these words:

"And the *peace* of God,
    which *transcends all understanding,*
        will guard your hearts and your minds
            in Christ Jesus."

*****

Chapter One
True

Seeking What Is True — Timeless and Priceless
By Everett (Bud) Hendrickson

Examples of people who sought what is true and those who didn't, span all time, starting with Adam and Eve and ending with us who are reading this book, plus those coming after we are gone. The personal examples throughout history of those who eagerly sought what was true, first enjoyed a relationship with God. That relationship motivated them to seek truth throughout their lifetimes. Blessings from God showed up as they lived.

One such person who offered a superb example of living what is true and reaping God's blessings was Joseph, whose story is recorded in the book of Genesis, Chapters 37-50.

Joseph's father, Jacob, loved Joseph, the youngest brother, more than his older siblings. Joseph had been born in his father's old age. Jacob loved Joseph, and had a special gift made for him; it was a beautiful robe. Joseph's older brothers hated him for the preferential treatment he enjoyed.

Long story short: Joseph had a dream and shared it with his brothers. It was about them harvesting wheat, and Joseph said that his sheave of wheat stood up, and the sheaves of wheat the others had gathered bowed down to his sheave. The brothers hated him even more since they surmised that Joseph thought he would be their king and reign over them.

Joseph's older brothers were highly envious of their youngest brother. In fact, they hated him so much they considered killing him, but some merchants were nearby so instead, they sold Joseph into slavery. Then the brothers killed a goat and put the blood on Joseph's beautiful robe the father had given him, and lied to their father that Joseph had been killed by a wild animal.

This one tragic life event alone would have crushed many people, but Joseph's character was strong and enduring. Although Joseph was sold into slavery, his heart stayed true to God's will. He was trustworthy to all, even his captors. This character influenced his Master and in a short time, Joseph was put in charge of everything his Master owned.

However, by being true he became subject to many lies which were told and spoken about him. Because of these, he was confined to prison again, and spent a couple of years there.

Joseph had been imprisoned for some time. He had gained favor with the warden, so much so that he was put in charge of all the prisoners. Soon thereafter the Pharaoh became offended by his cupbearer and chief baker. He had become angry with them and put them in the same prison where Joseph was being held.

While in prison the cupbearer and chief baker each experienced a dream. They both looked upset at this turn of events, and Joseph asked them why they looked so worried. They mentioned their dreams and that they could find no one who could interpret them. Joseph's response was that interpreting dreams was God's business, but he asked them to share their dreams.

Not only did Joseph interpret the dreams but both of his interpretations came true. One was that the Pharaoh's cupbearer would be restored to his position as chief cupbearer to the Pharaoh.

After the cupbearer had been reinstated, just as interpreted by Joseph, the Pharaoh had a dream his magicians and wise men could not interpret. The cupbearer remembered the young Hebrew who had interpreted his dream while in prison. The cupbearer told the Pharaoh that Joseph could interpret the dream his magicians could not. Pharaoh sent for Joseph and asked that his dream be interpreted.

Joseph said, "I cannot do it, but God will give you the answer you desire." So, Joseph interpreted the Pharaoh's dream. In doing so, he gained favor with Pharaoh because his interpretation was true and correct. One result was that Joseph became more trusted and he was given authority over Pharaoh's people and resources. He was rewarded because he had been true to God, himself, and others.

Toward the end of the story, we read that Joseph successfully managed Egypt in storing food for seven bountiful years before a severe famine was to hit the area. Many were going hungry due to lack of food when the famine came, including Joseph's father and brothers.

Joseph's brothers then traveled to Egypt to buy grain to bring back home, in order to keep the family from starving. When they arrived in Egypt, they didn't even know they were dealing with their younger brother, the one they had sold into slavery a long time ago.

Being true to God, Joseph showed mercy upon his family: he gave them grain *plus* their money back. Could Joseph been bitter and retaliated like so many seem to do today when lies and mistreatments occur? Yes, he could have been vengeful, but being true to God meant he was able to see how God had used his circumstances to save many lives, including those of his family.

How much do we desire to be more like Joseph and see how God can use us in challenging times if we stay true to His will?

Seeking What Is True — Timeless and Priceless

Seeking what is true today is as challenging as it has ever been. We are confronted 24/7 with multiple news media outlets, social media, and a host of online shows and podcasts. These drown us with information. Much of the time the so-called information sent out is composed of narratives that are complete opposites: 180 degrees from each other. Both cannot be true. The challenge for any listener is to determine what is actually accurate from all the narratives being broadcast to the masses.

~ Courtesy Google Images

Opposite narratives can and do divide most people, and we see this playing out in our current world. For example:

1. Today we have the pro-vaccinated crowd positioned against the unvaccinated crowd.
2. We see division about COVID: to shut down and isolate in order, supposedly, to "save" people from getting the virus, versus firms staying open, living normal lives, while protecting the vulnerable.

3. Even choices of therapeutics to treat COVID divide people.

I have lived through divisions in my neighborhood over these things. My wife and I chose not to get vaccinated; instead, we have chosen simple supplements like vitamin D, Zinc, and Vitamin C to support a healthy immune system to deal with COVID should we even get it.

We've also obtained Ivermectin as our proactive choice of a therapeutic. I'll say it was not easy to get!

I was called a stupid $#!& by one neighbor for not getting vaccinated. I explained to him that in some cases it may be best to be vaccinated, and honored his decision to do so, but with my low risk factor, concern over safety and lack of transparency for all to make an informed decision, I chose not to get vaccinated. I also mentioned that I would not be calling him a stupid $#!& for getting vaccinated. My neighbor said he felt this way because he cared for me.

I engaged in other discussions with other neighbors and all was okay until I talked about having Ivermectin for a therapeutic in case I got COVID. Her facial expression got angry and she said the conversation was over and she left abruptly. She did come back the next morning and apologize for her behavior but never wanted to learn why I made the decisions I did.

Seeking What Is True — Timeless and Priceless

Why are neighbors so strongly convicted on a narrative where no time or effort is spent to *understand* the other side and possibly find common ground? Why are these strongly held convictions more important than relationships? How many family, friend, and co-worker relationships are being negatively affected by putting one's preference over building relationships, seeking common ground, and understanding?

To be true to my conviction, I also lost a job because the firm for which I worked required me to be vaccinated. Many just told me, "Just take the jab." I made the decision even though I didn't know if other companies would even hire me. My wife and I even planned on a possible move from the state of Washington to Florida if needed. By being true to myself, God has blessed me with a great opportunity just 2.5 miles from where I live and vaccination is not required!

Another example in my small community, is a physician who has been treating COVID patients from the beginning with great success, using Ivermectin. The state has revoked his license to practice medicine. This doctor is cherished in the community, so much so that when someone gets COVID, people who know him and have been successfully treated by him send them his number so he can coach them on how to treat it based on their own situation.

Why would our government take a license from a person committed to helping people, who has a family to support, has experienced great success with his patients so they share his contact information with others, simply because he uses a treatment which has been proven that the worst side effects are nausea and diarrhea? Over the past five decades 4.8 billion doses have been administered safely. The government and main stream media want to tell us it is dangerous and is a horse de-wormer!

God is truth, God is love, and God is all knowing. Some of the ways I test for truth are these:

1. Since God will not marginalize me or call me names when someone else does, I know what any accuser is saying is not true.
2. God would never force me against my will, so when someone tries to compel me against my will, I also know that compulsion is not based on truth.

Here are some additional test examples:

1. Today, doctors are being marginalized and their licenses are revoked for treating patients with therapeutics.
2. If you feel that our last election process may have been stolen in the last election, you are accused of spreading the "Big Lie."
3. If you share information that the government or big tech deems you are engaging in misinformation, you are put in "social media jail."

4. For those who earn an income reporting on current events, they can be and often are removed, and defunded from their social platforms.
5. Wasn't the United States a country where we prided ourselves that we had the right to our own opinion, and that free speech was protected by the 1st Amendment of the Constitution?
6. What allows people to accept and believe totally opposite narratives since both cannot be true? How can this happen?

Mass Formation Psychosis

One phenomenon to investigate more closely, is Mass Formation Psychosis which has been studied and shared by a Dr. Mattis Desmet, Professor of Psychology – University of Ghent, Belgium. You could write a book just for this one topic alone. I will leave it up to the reader to research the topic in more detail, but I want to show what conditions need to be present and the effective actions to address it.

Mass Formation Psychosis emerges in society when four conditions are met:

1. Lack of a social bond
2. People experiencing life as meaningless or senseless
3. Free-floating anxiety and psychological discontent
4. Free-floating frustration and aggression

Throughout history segments of the population have experienced these four conditions. One obvious example of Mass Formation Psychosis is Germany in the 1930s and 1940s. Consider: how could many German people who were highly educated, liberal in the classic sense, and western-thinking people, go so crazy and do what they did to the Jews?

During the time before World War II, there was an economic crisis especially in European countries, following World War I. Millions of people worldwide lost their jobs and struggled to support and feed their families. Times were hard. People became desperate due to the economic hardships, and this desperation opened the door for political leaders with radical and extreme ideas, to gain power and influence by offering outrageous solutions to their country's problems.

One such leader that deceived the people of Germany with his inspiring speeches, promises to restore Germany back to economic prosperity, and international greatness was Adolf Hitler. One of his tactics was to blame the Jews for the economic crisis they were experiencing. With his people watching, Hitler ordered the brutal slaughtering of six million Jews.

Why didn't more people stand up against such evil of that time? The government with its force made it very difficult or harmed anyone who would speak up against the government's actions.

Seeking What Is True—Timeless and Priceless

~ Courtesy Google Images

Does this sound familiar with what has happened worldwide in the last two years (2020 and 2021) with COVID and the economic hardships felt and endured by so many?

So many have been isolated by lockdowns, forced to work from home, with institutions like hospitals not allowing loved ones to be with the people they love who are dealing with severe illness. This condition resulted in many going through recovery or death alone. I use this saying now with the crazy world in which we currently live, "It's not 2019 anymore"!

True: our Founding Fathers knew and understood the sinful nature of man. This was why our Representative Government was formed with the separation of powers in these three branches: Executive, Legislative, and Judicial. These three branches were formed to ensure that too much power was not vested in one person or branch of government.

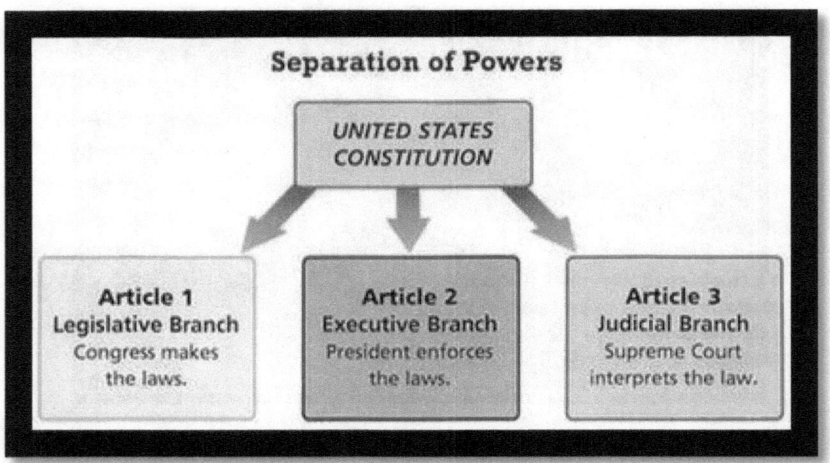

~ Courtesy Google Images

Our Federal Constitution is a *limiting* document for our Federal Government. Anything not stated in the Constitution is not a power of the Federal Government; rather, it is a State and Local governance issue. Our framers debated on how many people should be represented by an elected representative in Congress, and they felt the smaller the number, the more accountable they would be to their constituents. To allow the people to have more influence on how they are governed, more of our governance should be at the local and state level like the founding fathers intended it to be, with the Constitution restricting and limiting Federal Governance.

Seeking What Is True — Timeless and Priceless

~ Courtesy Google Images

Perhaps like you, I witness more executive orders from our current President, from 2021 to the present, regarding policy issues like vaccine mandates, the legality of COVID therapeutics, the delicensing of doctors who are trying to save their patients' lives with medicines which have a long history of safety, and a staunch resistance to look into 2020 election irregularities. Plus, I witness the labeling of anyone who supports the truth on any of these issues as spreading misinformation. Frankly, these observances have formed a huge awakening in me.

I am shocked as I now see what has been implemented right in front of us in bold and blatant efforts to take away our constitutional rights and steer us away from truth. My resolve? I am committed now more than ever to pass down truth to future generations on how to govern people for their prosperity and peace. Now more than ever I am grateful for the Godliness and fortitude our Founding Fathers who possessed the strength to pass down truth of governance to future generations.

Now is the time we need to stand for what is true and focus on our relationship with God, to build the resiliency to fend off the enemy of lies and deception in our world.

> Now is the time we need to stand for what is true and focus on our relationship with God, to build the resiliency to fend off the enemy of lies and deception in our world.

It is true that in the last few decades, technology has confined us, even as it may give us access to additional information. The last two years (2020 and 2021) have done much to isolate people even further from each other and their support systems. With the fear of dying from COVID or its long-term effects, shutdowns put so many in financial ruin.

Through no bad choices of their own, many normal endeavors that used to bring meaning to our lives have become not attainable due to shut downs and social limits. These major changes have affected our lives drastically.

Virtually all of them were changes over which we had no control.

Seeking What Is True — Timeless and Priceless

Startling statistics of our current world from the National Survey American Sociological Review:

1. 25% reported not one single close friend.
2. 75 million millennials age 18-27 reported more loneliness than in any other demographic, and one cause could be the social media world in which they grew up.
3. 50% now feel that their job is not meaningful.
4. Anxiety and frustrations about life have grown, with few knowing how to address these pressures.

~ *American Sociological Review* (ASR), the ASA's flagship journal, was founded in 1936 with the mission to publish original works of interest to the discipline of sociology in general, new theoretical developments, results of research that advance understanding of fundamental social processes, and important methodological innovations. Peer-reviewed and published bi-monthly, all areas of sociology are welcome, with emphasis on exceptional quality and general interest.

I would say we are in a prime time for Mass Formation Psychosis!

How does this affect us?

There is a section of our society that are in desperate need to socially connect. A narrative through mass media or social media that allows them to focus on issues they feel addresses their anxiety can make them vulnerable to accepting incorrect or unscientific information, and discourages them to being open to any other information.

This desire to connect to something or someone that they feel addresses their anxiety can make them radically blind to anything that goes against the narrative in which they believe.

This connection desire can become so compelling that they may be ethically convinced they are doing what is best for even those hurt by the narrative. Dr. Mattis Desmet states that about 20% to 30% of the population are thus affected.

How many times in the last couple of years have you seen evidence of these conditions occurring? Could this explain why we have such a divided society over government policies along with support from major media, big tech like Facebook, Twitter, and Google as they bombard us with their narratives and shut down or discredit any narratives counter to it?

How can anyone support the silencing of someone's right to share their opinion or position on a topic? Who is to determine what mis-information is? Are we better off when others decide what is to be shared with us and the masses?

I would never support the silencing of someone's voice even if they don't share the same views as mine. Real truth is like cream: it will rise to the top and prevail if given an equal chance to be shared.

Seeking What Is True—Timeless and Priceless

Fortunately, others are committed to finding out what is true and living it out in life. Dr. Mattis Desmet's data shows these number about 20% of the population.

Further, the Dr. Mattis Desmet data shows the remainder of about 40% of the population are fence sitters. These are the people who don't want to go against the current, and feel it is dangerous to go against the crowd.

How often do we see evidence today where pressure is put on people to conform to the main stream narrative, whatever it is? Fence sitters tend to remain silent and don't share or commit themselves on any topic. How often do you see evidence of people not spending enough time to seek truth or investigate real evidence provided to them?

The only way for truth to prevail is for the 20% who are committed to find out what is true and live it out in life to build a better and stronger self. Strength and courage will be developed that empowers them to find common ground and influence many with whom they come in contact, even regarding controversial issues.

God will give them the wisdom to share what is true in love, resulting in a more positive influence in their life and the lives of those they encounter. At first glance this can seem overwhelming and impossible, but with God nothing is impossible.

How do we make ourselves resilient to our world and receptive to the truth in every circumstance?

One Bible verse that comes to mind and was the scripture my wife and I used at our wedding. It's Ecclesiastes 4:12 (NIV):

> "Though one may be overpowered, two can defend themselves. A cord of three strands is not quickly broken."

By keeping God at the center of your relationship with your spouse, or a supportive friend in faith, a strength is built that makes us more resilient and spiritually healthy. Another verse to consider is Proverbs 27:17 "As iron sharpens iron so one man sharpens another." Just as there is benefit of rubbing two iron blades together to sharpen them, knives become more efficient in their task to cut and slice.

Likewise, two people with the Word of God sharpen one another wherever they fellowship or interact, to make them more effective in living God-centered lives. Strength is created.

This strength builds holistic health and allows relationships around you to be stronger and healthy.

This is represented by the next graphic:

Seeking What Is True — Timeless and Priceless

Influence Triangle

Just like the fire triangle where air and fuel are mixed correctly then introduced to an ignition source to produce fire/power, the influence triangle produces power in a similar way. You see, with the fire triangle, fuel and oxygen are present, but without the third element, an ignition source, no power is released.

The influence triangle is similar. God's truth and love are met with our action, which is like the ignition source, to produce the power/influence in your life and the lives of others. Your action will allow your life to be infused by the power of God and that power then can be released in the lives of others around you.

Start and remain strong in your cord of three strands with God. This should be your major focus and area of greatest influence.

Your biggest investment could be only in five or ten people with whom you have deep and regular relationships.

The power is that the people into whom you invest know and influence five or ten additional people separate from your support circle. Now the initial positive impact has reached twenty-five to 100 people.

~ Courtesy Google Images

With all of their combined strength and courage to find and live what is true, they then positively affect their next levels of five to ten people. This impact grows exponentially. Now you are up to potentially 1000 people being positively influenced by you. Your primary focus should be on being the best you that you can be. You will be empowered to invest in the small group closest to you.

Don't ever underestimate the influence you have in focusing and investing in a small group of people. As you build a stronger and better you, that effort alone will be a potential catalyst for thousands more.

Seeking What Is True — Timeless and Priceless

A change in the world starts with each of us becoming a better God-centered person, and thereby becoming the best example we can be to others. The key is to keep the cord of three stands connected as we go through life. We can develop the holistic health to positively influence others around us.

> The key is to keep the cord of three stands connected as we go through life. We can develop the holistic health to positively influence others around us.

Once people are committed to what is true, they build a solid foundation through their faith in God, with themselves, and with family and friends.

We need to go in love and tell the truth to all we contact. We need to package the evidence of what is true in ways to influence them to accept and support what is true. If the people with whom you connect understand the love and care you have for them as people, just as God does, they will be more open to listen and find the common ground that will allow action that will meet the needs of many others.

Now more than ever we need soldiers carrying the message of what is true to their family, friends, co-workers, and neighbors, including those who may be straddling the fence of truth and non-truth, if we ever are able to get our families, communities, country, and world heathy again.

Bud Hendrickson

Truth packaged in God-centered love will influence others to be open and receptive to what is true.

Our most impactful ministry and testimony will come from our deepest scars. Who better to support and encourage someone who has lost a child or another loved one than someone who has successfully gone through that life event? Who better to be by the side of someone who is dealing with an addiction than someone who has lived through an addiction, and has come out on the other side even stronger through their reliance on God?

Don't let a hurt go to waste; put it to work for God. See the miracles God can do through you.

*****

~ Bud and Kristin Hendrickson, Engagement Portrait,
Powers Photography, June, 2019

How Bud Hendrickson and Glen Aubrey know each other:

From Bud:

How I met Glen:

Glen's brother-in-law, Keith, was a friend of mine. Our children attended school together. I had shared with him some of my concerns with issues at work. On the job we would train on conflict resolution and communication, but the employees didn't always apply the training.

I consistently felt the need to go back one step and coach on the benefits of good conflict resolution and communication, extending not only at work but also in personal life application. Keith introduced me to Glen in the year 2000.

Later that same year Glen spoke at our company's off-site meeting about relationships. Since that time, Glen as trained and consulted with two other companies for whom I've worked. Additionally, Glen consulted in my church to help develop programming arts teams. My wife, Nancy, and I had been attending this church for twenty years.

Glen's and my friendship and respect for each other has grown over time. This relationship resulted in me writing and publishing my first book with his guidance. Plus, I have been a contributing author for two others books of his authorship.

The book I have written, published by Glen Aubrey and Creative Team Publishing was this: *Enjoy Greater Results with Less Effort * Build A Better You*
(www.greaterresultslesseffort.com)

The two books in which I contributed a chapter:

1. ***God's Plan Unfolding * Strength and Renewal in Times of Crisis*** www.godsplanunfolding.com
2. ***Whatever Is True * Return to Holistic Health*** www.whateveristruehealth.com

We may have grown up in different parts of the country, developed different skills along our life's journeys, but our love for God and the value we put on people are in direct and correct alignment with each other. This alignment has been the foundation for the great relationship we enjoy.

~ Bud Hendrickson, April-May, 2022

From Glen:

Bud Hendrickson and I have been personal and professional acquaintances for a long time. We know each other well, and we know each other's families. Bud is an engineer with a passion for ministry. A wonderful combination!

One of my profound joys is to be Bud's book publisher. Creative Team Publishing (CTP) is honored to have Bud and his book represented in our catalog. Please access www.creativeteampublishing.com.

His most recent book is: ***Enjoy Greater Results with Less Effort * Build a Better You***. Based on his **Ten Bedrock Truths**, his message is solid, truthful, uplifting, practical, and Biblical.

Please see this website and order this book: www.greaterresultslesseffort.com. It's a life-changing, refreshing perspective on our dependence on God coupled with our responsibilities as His followers.

I strongly recommend Bud and his writings to you!

~ Glen Aubrey, April-May, 2022

*****

Chapter Two
Noble

Politics and Media
By John Culea

The Apostle Paul was divinely inspired in his New Testament writings and would have made a great political consultant, commentator, and journalism professor. His exhortations in Philippians 4:8 to think about *Whatever Is True* is a template for the way things ought to be in politics and the media.

But thinking and *doing* whatever is noble, pure, lovely, admirable, excellent, or praiseworthy is an altogether different life model.

*****

For 31 years, from 1969 to 1999, I was a television news anchor/reporter, beginning in Phoenix, Arizona at KTAR-TV, and then working at KGTV in San Diego, WLS-TV in Chicago, before returning to San Diego at KFMB-TV for twenty years.

John Culea

John Culea, live news reporting, San Diego backdrop

In the late 1980s I taught broadcast journalism at Point Loma Nazarene University. Throughout the course, I used Philippians 4:8, and also Ephesians 5:11, quoted here:

> [11] Have nothing to do with the fruitless deeds of darkness, but rather expose them.

Plus, I used Colossians 3:12, quoted here:

> [12] Therefore, as God's chosen people, holy and dearly loved, clothe yourselves with compassion, kindness, humility, gentleness and patience.

Politics and Media

It's called "speaking the truth, in love." (This is a reference to Ephesians 4:15). <u>The verse above contains powerful guidelines for how to report a news story</u>. The verse should be the basis for investigative journalism and, oh, by the way, the list gives us instructions as to how politicians should lead their lives and it's for those who are not necessarily in politics.

*****

After my career in television news ended, I worked for San Diego County Supervisor Bill Horn as his media and communications director for ten years, before retiring in 2001. I was told by some people that by going from news into politics, I had joined the "dark side."

Actually, one of the reasons I was hired was that I knew how the news media worked and used that knowledge and experience to help the Supervisor get his message to his constituents.

There were problems dealing with members of the media who had their own agenda. For instance, a weekly newspaper *San Diego City Beat* on May 26, 2010, featured a front-page photo of the Supervisor being dropped in a toilet bowl with the words:

John Culea

FLUSH BILL HORN: WHAT TO DO WITH A COUNTY SUPERVISOR WHO REALLY STINKS

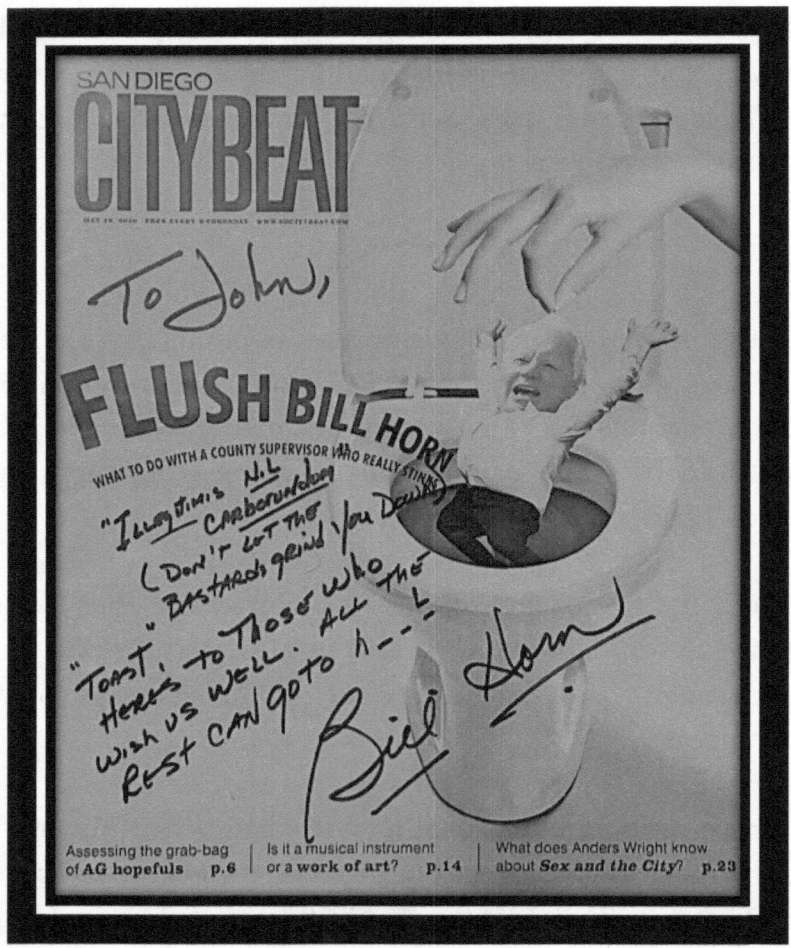

The Supervisor often asked me why some in the media hated him, and I always reminded him of the things that were working against him; namely, he was a Christian, pro-life, pro-business, pro-military, a conservationist and not an environmentalist, he was rich, and he was fat. Other than needing to lose weight, I encouraged him to remain true to his values because that was why people voted for him.

John Culea and Bill Horn, 2012

Flagpole National Day of Prayer County Administration Headquarters Downtown, San Diego

One event Supervisor Horn hosted each year always brought media criticism and public praise. In May 1999, Bill was the first elected official in San Diego County to invite county employees to join him at the county administration headquarters flagpole for a group prayer at noon on the National Day of Prayer. The first year he did it, the only people at the flagpole were the Supervisor, his chief of staff, Joan Wonsley, and a few staff members. They began praying and were watched from windows of the county building by employees. Soon, people began joining them and a tradition had begun.

Supervisor Bill Horn at "Prayer at the Flagpole"

I was hired two years later and handled what was needed for the event including having a proclamation issued by the Supervisor honoring the National Day of Prayer, and preparing an email that went to all county employees inviting them to attend.

It was made clear that it would be held on their free time during the lunch break between 12:30 p.m. and 1 p.m. The proclamation was a way to satisfy County Counsel attorneys who were nervous about having a "religious" event on county property.

Politics and Media

The Official Proclamation

The last prayer at the flagpole event I organized was May 5, 2011. The proclamation contained eight "**WHEREAS'**" including: "**WHEREAS**, the National Day of Prayer (NDP) is a vital part of our heritage, as evidenced by the first call to prayer in 1775 by the Continental Congress that asked the colonies to pray for wisdom in forming our nation; and **WHEREAS**, in 1988, President Ronald Reagan permanently set the National Day of Prayer as the first Thursday of every May and every president since then has signed a proclamation encouraging all Americans to pray on this day:

NOW THEREFORE, BE IT PROCLAIMED by Chairman Bill Horn and all members of the San Diego County Board of Supervisors on the 5th day of May, 2011 as the **NATIONAL DAY OF PRAYER**, and in honor of its 60th anniversary, do hereby declare this day to be **"NATIONAL DAY OF PRAYER"** throughout San Diego County.

National Day of Prayer, San Diego County

Politics and Media

Each year we had a four-piece brass ensemble from the downtown Salvation Army there to play gospel songs. Attendance varied from 50 to 75 people and many spontaneously prayed for the nation, our county, and our city.

The loudest critic of the event each year was Logan Jenkins, a columnist with the *San Diego Union* newspaper. On May 3, 2001, a headline for his column gives you an idea where his heart was:

Day of Prayer: Politicians get to play the piety card

Included in his column:

"The National Day of Prayer has dawned. The 50th annual open-air observance of full-court Christian supplication.

I know, I know. I'm not supposed to say Christian. Those of ANY faith are invited to pray in public today. So goes the it's-everyone's-party line …

As the grandson of a Presbyterian minister, I'm not in the least put off by Christian prayer, in closets or on courthouse steps. All I ask is that we be more than half honest about the role of politics in prayer on the public square …

It's worth noting that the National Day of Prayer (NDP), the first Thursday in May, either coincides with or follows

May Day, when the Soviets used to strut their missiles on Red Square ...

In North County, no one has played the piety card more often than our own Supervisor Bill Horn. Along with property rights, godliness is his strong suit. The good Sunday suit ...

Last week, Horn--now Chairman Horn--sent out an advisory, reviewing the long, distinguished history of public prayer in America. The subhead of the letter reads, "Chairman invites people of all faiths to meet him at the county flagpole to pray."

As explained earlier, everybody understands the "all-faiths" feint. The likelihood of Jews or Buddhists joining Horn's group at 7 a.m. today is slight to nil."

*****

Remember, that mean-spirited and snarky column was written more than two decades ago, but as it turned out, Jenkins' hostility was a tame preview of the media and political environment in which we live today.

In January 2019, Supervisor Horn was termed out of office and the County of San Diego stopped the National Day of Prayer flagpole event. If other supervisors wanted to continue

Politics and Media

the tradition, it did not happen, but County Counsel was relieved to be rid of the event.

Prayer at the county flagpole was one of the few remaining rays of light in a public world increasingly hostile to the gospel. Recently, the conditions we live in were eloquently explained by Dr. John Greene, senior pastor for nearly 50 years at Harmony Hill Baptist Church in our new hometown of Lufkin, Texas.

Dr. John Greene, Senior Pastor
Harmony Hill Baptist Church
Lufkin, Texas

Perhaps you have experienced the remarkable feeling that I have had over the years of how a pastor's Sunday message seems to be directed straight at you. Such was the case April 3, 2022, when pastor Greene listed five ways the world is increasingly hostile to the gospel; insight that fit perfectly with the theme of this chapter.

He said followers of Christ must learn to live in the tension of hostility to the gospel and at the same time know the desperate need for the gospel, which alone can rescue people from hell. Using Romans 1:18-32, pastor Greene outlined God's abandonment of a nation when five things begin to happen that cause the world to marginalize Christians.

a. Rejecting the Bible

At a news conference in Turkey, April 2009, President Barrack Obama said Americans, "do not consider ourselves a Christian nation ..."

Rejecting the Bible as our national authority leads to:

b. Morality being turned upside down

Romans 1:26-28 (NIV):

[26] Because of this, God gave them over to shameful lusts. Even their women exchanged natural sexual relations for unnatural ones. [27] In the same way the men also abandoned natural relations with women and were inflamed with lust for one another. Men committed shameful acts with other men, and received in themselves the due penalty for their error. [28] Furthermore, just as they did not think

Politics and Media

it worthwhile to retain the knowledge of God, so God gave them over to a depraved mind, so that they do what ought not to be done.

We live in times when most of the media and many politicians have a national acceptance of homosexuality, sex outside of marriage, and they espouse that abortion is good.

In California, Assembly Bill 223 by Assemblywoman Buffy Wicks (D-Oakland), legalizes infanticide in an abortion bill to expand the killing of babies past the moment of birth up to weeks after.

Meantime, Colorado Governor Jared Polis signed a new pro-abortion law that denies all rights and protections to babies prior to birth.

With this, there is almost universal

    c. Demand for tolerance

Men and women in congress, judges, presidents, and Hollywood not only encourage homosexuality, gay marriage, and abortion, but demand tolerance and special treatment for people deemed to be economically marginalized.

In Palm Springs, California, a new $200,000 tax-supported pilot program is in force that gives transgender and nonbinary residents a universal basic income (UBI) of $900.00

per month solely on the basis of their identity. (Non-binary identities fall under the transgender umbrella, since non-binary people typically identify with a gender that is different from their assigned sex.)

They receive a UBI with no regard for earnings, whether they are unemployed or earn more than $100,000 per year.

According to local leaders, the program was started because transgender and nonbinary people are, in their opinion, economically marginalized.

A mandate for tolerance can also be found in the spreading religion of Critical Race Theory (CRT). *Lighthouse Trails Publication* (LTP) explains that it is a movement that began in the 1980s by lawyers and social activists. People are put in specific identity groups (e.g., whites, blacks, lesbians, feminists, genders). Each group is categorized as either "oppressor" or "oppressed."

LTP has found that, "Those who embrace Critical Race Theory believe CRT is going to help end racial tensions and create a more loving world. On the contrary, it is going to cause animosity, suspicion, anger, and all the things that are the opposite of God's love that is described in (the Bible)."

Politics and Media

Pressure to be tolerant leads to:

    d. Intolerance of the gospel

One consequence is that marriage is redefined. If Christian bakers won't make cakes with two men or women at the top, they are labeled "intolerant" and open to lawsuits.

Speaking the truth becomes bigotry. These are times when it is wrong to say something is wrong. And for those who do stand for Biblical truth, Jesus warned to expect:

    e. Persecution of the gospel

The final step of a nation turning from God is silencing people talking about the gospel.

Romans 1:32

> [32] Although they know God's righteous decree that those who do such things deserve death, they not only continue to do these very things but also approve of those who practice them.

The Old and New Testaments have many warnings that believers will be hated by everyone because of God's name.

In Matthew 5:11, Jesus said, 11 "Blessed are you when people insult you, persecute you and falsely say all kinds of evil against you because of me."

Pastor Greene did more than detail the world we live in; he gave words to remember and live by in a world hostile to the gospel. He warned of the danger of making people who are about to die and perish in hell to become the enemy. We cannot turn men and women hostile to the gospel into our enemies and objects of hatred. We cannot hate lost people. Jesus, in Matthew 5, said to "Love your enemies" and "Love your neighbor as yourself." But in Matthew 10:16, He also told believers, "I am sending you out like sheep among wolves. Therefore, be as shrewd as snakes and as innocent as doves."

One lesson I quickly learned with Supervisor Horn was that in politics you cannot go to war on every issue and expect the outcome to be exactly what you want. Fundamental principles should not be sacrificed, but compromise is needed to get things done.

You will not find the list of characteristics in the **Whatever Is True** passage in most politicians today or for that matter, in much of society. True Nobility is lacking.

When it comes to trust, our political leaders in Washington rate right down there with used car salesmen and the media. A 2021 *Pew Research* study revealed only about one-quarter of

Politics and Media

Americans say they can trust the government in Washington to do what is right "just about always" (2%), or "most of the time" (22%).
~ Original Source:
https://www.pewresearch.org/politics/2021/05/17/public-trust-in-government-1958-2021/

And what about the media that reports on events in Washington, D.C.? A 2021 *Reuters Institute* survey found the U.S. media is the least trustworthy of 46 countries in the world. Supporting those results is a 2019 *Axios/Survey Monkey* poll reported by *The Hill* in 2021. It found that nearly 8 in 10 independent voters said they believed that news organizations report news "they know to be fake, false, or purposely misleading." Ninety-two percent of Republicans felt the same way, as did a majority of Democrats.

An example of deception is the Internet search engine, Google. In 2019, I published a book about people using "fillers" when they speak. "Fillers" are meaningless words, phrases, or sounds that are employed instead of a pause or hesitation in speech. While doing research for my book, ***Ah, I mean, like, well, so, you know, why do people talk this way? Felony assault on the English language***, I saw how Google's search engine is programmed with heavy liberal bias. When I entered the words "worst word fillers from Donald Trump," seconds later there were 265,000 results. The search results included an article from *Vanity Fair* "Experts: Trump's Speaking Style 'Raises Questions About His Brain Health.'"

Conversely, when I entered "worst language fillers from ultra-liberal Alexandria Ocasio-Cortez," whose speeches and media interviews are replete with fillers, the number of Google results about the New York Representative were nine.

In April 2020, after living in San Diego for 40 years (35 in the same house), my wife Patti and I moved from San Diego, California to the small east Texas city of Lufkin. I wrote about that in *Goodbye California: Why It Was Time to Go and How We Did It*. We were happy to escape the liberal bias of *The San Diego Union* newspaper.

When it came to the *San Diego Union*, the phrase **"Whatever Is True"** was often "usually fake."

Unfortunately, I soon found you can't get away from it.

That summer of 2020, *The Lufkin Daily News* printed an Associated Press story after President Trump spoke at Mount Rushmore on July 4. This was the original article used by *The Lufkin Daily News*.
~ Original Source Credit:
https://apnews.com/article/10793013ab9d6febaf896b2bd25ec62a

Politics and Media

At Mt. Rushmore, President Trump touts importance of historical figures

Associated Press
Jul 4, 2020 Updated Jul 4, 2020

(There was a photograph of the President and First Lady on a stage. He was saluting and the First Lady had her right hand over her heart. The sculpted figures of Washington, Jefferson, Teddy Roosevelt, and Lincoln were behind them. In the distance, the Blue Angels were doing a flyover.)

Photo: *Lufkin Daily News and New York Times*

Here are the first two paragraphs of the story as it appeared in *The Lufkin Daily News*:

John Culea

MOUNT RUSHMORE NATIONAL MEMORIAL, S.D. (AP)

At the foot of Mount Rushmore on the eve of Independence Day, President Donald Trump made a direct appeal to disaffected voters four months before Election Day, accusing protesters of engaging in a "merciless campaign to wipe out our history."

The president dug further Friday, appealing to an electorate battered by a pandemic, and wounded by racial injustice following the high-profile killings of Black people. He zeroed in on the desecration by some protesters of monuments and statues across the country.

*****

I was outraged at the blatant bias in the report and sent the following letter to the newspaper's publisher and editor.

"This morning I read an article in the *Lufkin Daily News* in our new home of Lufkin, Texas. We are receiving the newspaper through a four-week gift subscription.

In the paper there was an article from the Associated Press by Stephen Groves and Darlene Superville on President Trump's speech at Mount Rushmore. Here are the first two sentences:

Politics and Media

"At the foot of Mount Rushmore on the eve of Independence Day, President Donald Trump made a direct appeal to disaffected white voters four months before Election Day, accusing protestors who have pushed for racial justice of engaging in a 'merciless campaign to wipe out our history.'

The president dug further into American divisions on Friday, offering a discordant tone to an electorate battered by a pandemic and wounded by racial injustice following the high-profile killings of Black people. He zeroed in on the desecration by some protestors of monuments and statues across the country that honor those who have benefited from slavery, including some past presidents."

My comments:

1. President Trump never mentioned 'white voters.'
2. Are only 'white voters' feeling 'disaffected?'
3. And what exactly does 'disaffected' mean?
4. Voters are feeling many emotions, including repulsion of what is proposed by so-called 'progressives,' a continued litany of failure by most big cities controlled by Democrat politicians and fear of what would happen if Joe Biden wins the Presidency in November.
5. The reporters editorialized by saying 'the president dug further into American divisions.' Their opinion, certainly not mine.

6. The reporters then wrote that he offered 'a discordant tone' but never mentioned that Mr. Trump continually emphasized the greatness of America.
7. The writers capitalized 'Black people' but did not do so when referring to 'white voters.'
8. My conclusion: "you don't have to look very far to realize that bias is very much alive and not so very well in our media."

*****

The newspaper responded to the email the same day when Publisher Keven Todd wrote the following:

Sat., Jul 4, 2:52 PM
Keven Todd
To me, Jeff [Jeff Pownall, Managing Editor, *Lufkin Daily News*]

"Thanks, John, I appreciate your thoughtful comments."

*****

I wondered what would be done, and had to wait until the following Wednesday for the newspaper's next edition.

Politics and Media

I opened the paper and saw that my letter had been printed.

> never mentioned continually emphasized the greatness of America.
>
> The writers capitalized "Black people" but did not do so when referring to "white voters."
>
> My conclusion: You don't have to look very far to realize that bias is very much alive and not so very well in our media.
>
> — John Culea, Lufkin

I was pleased that my viewpoint was aired. But then I got a huge shock when I looked to the left of the page and saw the newspaper's editorial.

Politics and Media

The newspaper agreed with me that the article was biased and what made it even more remarkable and rare was that the publisher said the newspaper "showed poor judgment in running it."

I sent the publisher and managing editor an email that included the following:

"Hello Keven and Jeff: Thank you for printing my letter this morning regarding the AP story about President Trump's speech at Mount Rushmore. I appreciate the opportunity to express my opinion in writing on the bias of the reporters who wrote the story.

I also admire you for admitting that it was poor judgment for your newspaper to use the story and was pleasantly surprised to see that expressed in a long editorial."

*****

I thought the small victory for truth was over, until I further researched the AP article. I discovered a curious difference in the original Associated Press story that was in *The Lufkin Daily News* and the one that came up on an Internet search for the same story.

Above the AP headline on the Internet is a different photograph. This one shows a closeup of the figures on Mount Rushmore and next to them is an equally large photograph of President Trump looking up with a smirk on his face, the clear implication being that he would like to have his bust be part of the national memorial.

Associated Press photo

And when I compared the two articles; one in *The Lufkin Daily News* and the other from the Associated Press, I saw major changes beginning with the headline.

At Mount Rushmore, Trump digs deeper into nation's divisions

(The AP story has a negative opinionated headline about the President while the one chosen by *The Lufkin Daily News* was positive toward the nation)

Politics and Media

By STEPHEN GROVES, DARLENE SUPERVILLE and AAMER MADHANI
July 4, 2020

MOUNT RUSHMORE NATIONAL MEMORIAL, S.D. (AP)

"At the foot of Mount Rushmore and on the eve of Independence Day, President Donald Trump dug deeper into America's divisions by accusing protesters who have pushed for racial justice of engaging in a 'merciless campaign to wipe out our history.'

The president, in remarks Friday night at the South Dakota landmark, offered a discordant tone to an electorate battered by a pandemic and seared by the recent high-profile killings of Black people. He zeroed in on the desecration by some demonstrators of monuments and statues across the country that honor those who have benefited from slavery, including some past presidents.

Four months from Election Day, his comments amounted to a direct appeal to the political base, including many disaffected white votes, that carried him to the White House in 2016."

*****

(The word 'disaffected' was shifted to the third paragraph in the revised Internet story; one example of a story that seemed to be continuously evolving.)

*****

Earlier I mentioned the end of my TV news career when I began working for Supervisor Horn. Before that happened, there was a gap of 14 months when I did not have a job. While I was never depressed, I was surprised at the length of time that passed.

I interviewed for several jobs and was a finalist to be press secretary for the Mayor of San Diego, special assistant for a County Sheriff and special assist for the County District Attorney. The Lord was good because the DA lost the next election, the guy who got the sheriff's job only lasted two years, and the mayor resigned from office after a scandal involving the city's debt-ridden pension fund. Before he left office, *Time* magazine named him one of the three worst mayors of a major U.S. city.

God's timing for me was perfect and during more than a year being out of work, I was able to pray more, study God's Word more, and wait upon the Lord for what He wanted me to do. I walked a lot and one day, unshaven and dressed in old clothes, I was making my way to the post office. I often rehearsed what I was going to say in an upcoming interview and also prayed out loud for what the day was going to bring.

I must have looked a sight, talking to myself, and dressed like a bum.

As I was walking on the sidewalk, a bird flew into the grill of a passing truck and bounced to the curb, DOA. How sad. I decided to bury it but first had to walk to the post office. So, I picked up the dead bird and soon spotted a grocery cart someone had discarded along the sidewalk.

Knowing I was headed past a supermarket, I decided to push it there. Just then, I saw cardboard boxes that had flown out of a vehicle, so I put all of the trash in the shopping cart and continued walking. Ahead of me was a young woman with two little children. She looked over her shoulder at me and in an excited voice said, "Oh, look, kids. How exciting, it's John Culea from Channel 8 News!"

With the children staring at the dead bird in my hand and my shopping cart filled with cardboard, I probably looked like a candidate for County Mental Health but thanked the young woman for recognizing me and told her I was not with the station anymore. As for the dead bird in my hand, I told the kids I was going to bury it later. I still was months from working for the Supervisor but used the story several times at churches I spoke at to encourage others.

*****

With the current political climate in America today, it is easy to give up, thinking nothing can be done to change our nation's direction. It is also difficult to follow Paul's admonition to do more than *think* about "whatever is right." When a Supreme Court nominee says she cannot give the definition of a woman, the Walt Disney Company eliminates the words "ladies," "gentlemen," "boys," and "girls" in its theme parks to not offend people who are not sure about their gender, and U.S. passports can be marked "X" as a person's gender, all in the name of woke diversity, the battle, while still belonging to the Lord, seems lost.

One of America's most articulate commentators on politics and the media is Victor Davis Hanson of Stanford's Hoover Institution. As a former TV news reporter, I marvel at every interview Hanson gives. Unlike other interview subjects, he is almost never interrupted while talking and his interviews last much longer than is the norm. The reason is he always has something profound to say and does so with brilliant clarity.

Says Hanson: civil laws are not necessarily binding anymore and wokeness is the new religion, growing faster and larger than Christianity.

*****

The words of Philippians 4:8 should mean something. But today, the words true, noble, right, pure, lovely, admirable, excellent, or praiseworthy are shaped to fit what is humanistically and politically comfortable. Doing that is a large segment of Americans who consider themselves superior. To them there are no absolutes. Truth is relative. They are among the social and intellectual elite and they call themselves "progressives."

But progressives have a truckload of problems to deal with when they reject the Bible's perfect and absolute truth.

Psalm 19:7, NIV:

> 7 The law of the LORD is perfect, refreshing the soul. The statutes of the LORD are trustworthy, making wise the simple.

Psalm 119:142, (NIV):

> 142 Your righteousness is everlasting and your law is true.

One consequence is that the word "progressive" has brought unintended political resistance. Some liberal candidates who identify as "progressives" are finding that voters see the mess our country is in today and hold them responsible for what has happened. They want candidates who are anti-establishment and have an against-the-system sentiment. The shifting whims of political reality have caused some "progressives" to no longer use the term. Instead, they use the word "populist;" a person who tries to appeal to ordinary people who feel the established elite have ignored their concerns.

But no matter how much lipstick you put on a pig, it's still a pig.

*****

America is bombarded on all sides by wokeness, Critical Race Theory, transgender mania, hedonism, and social isolation brought about by a government over-reaction to COVID. Our nation appears to be more divided than ever, and not just politically. People are angry about everything. There seems to be a growing climate of hate. Today what is news and how it is reported (or manipulated) reflect an alarming change in much of America. Perhaps the most unsettling reality is that many people making the news, especially in California, the state we left two years ago, love to hate.

The Beatles in 1967 sang, "All you need is love." Today's chorus from the left is "All we want to do is hate."

This is definitely *not* Noble.

I first realized how dramatic the shift was that had happened when my wife and I took a trip to Texas in December, 2019. The difference between what we had seen in

Politics and Media

California and what we discovered in Texas was astounding. We saw firsthand that in large part, Texans love their country, state, families, and their neighbors. There was no shortage of "Yes, sir," "No, ma'am," "Mr. John," "Miss Patti," and "Have a blessed day." Many Texans also have a deep love for God and welcome opportunities to share what they have with the needy. Just about wherever we went, Texans were cordial, unpretentious, optimistic, and projected a joy not seen that much in California.

Paul wrote about much more than "Whatever is true." Before you can think or put in practice whatever is true, noble, right, pure, lovely, admirable, excellent, or praiseworthy, <u>there must be love</u>. In all his writings, Paul instructed believers to walk in love, to let love be without pretense, clinging to what is good, to be patient, and unify. That is glaringly absent from the political and social scene today.

In truth, there is much to love about our country. For a while, our economy had never been better. People of all descriptions were employed in record numbers. Our military was being restored to its once-dominant force. The leader of our nation had a deep commitment to the right to life, preserving our Second Amendment, and protecting religious liberty. Federal judges were being appointed who were true to the Constitution and the U.S. Supreme Court vacancies were filled with originalists.

Unless things drastically change, we may never see those times again. But "never" is a long time. And we have a God who is totally in control. We know how the story is going to end. We just don't know when He is going to write earth's final chapter.

Let's return to the true Biblical Nobility of knowing right from wrong, and Biblical truth from humanistic opinion.

*****

How John Culea and Glen Aubrey met:

From John:

Glen,

I cannot give you the exact year when we met, but it would have likely been in the 80s with YFC (Youth for Christ) and Executive Director, Gene French. We went to Community Bible Church (CBC) when they met in Scripps Ranch in the early 80s.

Then, we had a closer association when you did consulting work for CBC after the church moved to Mira Mesa. Patti and I were there for five years. Following a difficult experience with the church (not related to a former pastor, and after he resigned) we returned to Emmanuel Faith in Escondido before coming to Texas.

You asked about my books. To date, I have written twenty-two. I think my book that has sold the most was ***One-Way or Round Trip: Women Flight Attendants and Troops During the Vietnam War.*** That book was Patti's idea, and her time as a flight attendant in Vietnam is part of the book.

Infamy to Injustice: Liberty's Shame also did pretty well. That historical fiction is the story of 1,100 Japanese who were forced to leave San Diego after Pearl Harbor. They were taken to Santa Anita Racetrack and then to Poston, Arizona near Kingman.

The Hub Shootout: San Diego's Unbelievable Four-Hour Firefight was my first nonfiction book and it sold well, especially to the San Diego law enforcement community.

Light the Night, Target Tombstone, SanDiegoland, and the three books on our move to Texas have also sold a few copies. I think that the current Handel book will also do well.

All can be purchased on Amazon.
~ https://www.amazon.com/Books-John-Culea/s?rh=n%3A283155%2Cp_27%3AJohn+Culea

~John Culea, April, 2022

From Glen:

A friendly rivalry existed, at least in my estimation, between ABC Channel 10 news, featuring anchor Carol Le Beau, and CBS Channel 8 news, featuring anchor John Culea. One of my goals in working with Youth for Christ (YFC) as Media, Music, and Television Director, was to join Carol and John on the same YFC TV program; both of them were staunch supporters of YFC, dedicated servants of Christ, and personal friends. The goal of joining them never occurred … I think because it was not possible to have both news anchors on the same show.

Nevertheless, they showed their love for teenagers, YFC's work with them, and their commitment for Christ, for which I will always be grateful.

~ Glen Aubrey, April 2022

*****

Patti and John Culea, Texas, 2022

Chapter Three
Right

Fixed on Doing Right
By Pastor James Patton

Why must we fix, dwell, and focus our thoughts on what is right?

Mom said it best: "It is far easier to just tell the truth and do right, rather than work to not get tangled in a web of wrong."

Have you noticed a truth that "where the mind goes the body follows?" As a volunteer Co-Pastor of a church located in a Skilled Nursing Facility, I have the privilege of witnessing it constantly. I have seen hurting people who were sick and tired of living, be transformed almost instantly when they changed their focus and framework.

Thinking right is the key to success in any endeavor, whether it is health, business, sports, or relationships. That is not just my opinion: there are countless studies and examples before us that offer proof of this maxim. Being a champion or chump is a matter of choice and commitment.

Pastor James Patton

> Think right to be right.

> "The destiny of a civilized humanity depends more than ever on the moral forces it is capable of generating."
> ~ Albert Einstein www.Journals.UChicago.Edu>Doi>Pdf

What is right?

A bank president once told me that the best way to learn to spot counterfeits is to learn to recognize what is right, because, once you know the key points of what is real, then anything else is wrong. It was the same principle when I worked in security, checking ID.

For example, the paper on the bills is smooth except only the jackets of the different presidents are in raised ink, so if the etching does not match, then the bill is bogus. If the watermark portrait does not match the printed portrait: bogus again. Driver licenses also have several specific security features.

Fixed on Doing Right

The point is: if you know what is real and do a basic check, you don't have to keep track of all the new ways to create or be conned by fakes. It is the same for other truths in life also.

> "Worse than being blind is to be able to see but not have any vision."

~ Helen Keller.

The Merriam-Webster Dictionary defines Right this way: In morals and religion, just; equitable; accordant to the standard of truth and justice or the will of God. That alone is *right* in the sight of God, which is consonant to his will or law; this being the only perfect standard of truth and justice.

~ Merriam-Webster, 1828

Let's start with that.

Who decides what is right?

Absolute Owner Authority. God Almighty says it is so. God sees when someone substitutes a replacement for the true God, as their god. Isn't it interesting that there is always an authority we are submitted to, even if it is anarchy?

As citizens, or even "visitors just passing through" we can either comply, or pay the consequences.

Believe it or not, people exist who don't believe in gravity. (And consequences follow!)

GIGO (Garbage In, Garbage Out) is an Information Technology term that applies in life because if we build on fallacies not facts then we get more multipliers of what we started with. That is why it is necessary to check out the source material or credentials of the experts upon whom we rely. Are they credentialed experts in this area? Do they have a key bias or are they recognized as a neutral? What is the historical and current context of the "The Whole Truth?" What is the reality beneath the rhetoric? In my humble opinion: The more it matters: the more it matters.

As Christians, we are blessed to be allowed the opportunity to choose to believe in God as revealed and recorded in the Bible, and The Holy Spirit. Obviously, I am not an expert; however, I am an eyewitness, sharing what I have experienced. For a quick and easy overview of detailed objective documentation on the authenticity and authority of the Bible, please read *Evidence That Demands A Verdict* by Josh McDowell.

KEY POINT: Billions of people from many backgrounds and faiths agree on what is morally right. This is about relationships, not religion. These concepts supersede cliques.

Kelvin Howard, a U.S. Marine ("once a Marine always a Marine"), shared with me that before deploying, everyone gets in a line and does a "Buddy Check" of everything about the Marine ahead of them in the line: ensuring everything is perfect (the one in front circles back to check the one in back).

Fixed on Doing Right

We as believers need to do the same thing. It is not a matter of opinion or option. Survival starts with simply aligning with the authoritative standard. Every morning I call some of my closest contacts and do a mental/spiritual "buddy check" and they do the same for me. We don't always know what is ahead, so we have to be fully prepared. We do reconnaissance and based on reports that help us get ready. We can't always see what we might have missed; but by us trusting each other and taking care of each other, we all win.

That does not mean the blind leading the blind into a conflict; it means we get ready, reliable, and right *beforehand*. We have to be careful whose report we believe.

The bogus news is like that **Hee Haw** song: "… doom, despair, and agony on me …" and that is what follows when we pay attention to the gossip. But if we receive and think about the Gospel, which is the "Good News," and allow it to be implemented in us, it empowers us to believe and achieve. "We have to get our head right or we go out to battle, leaving our helmet at home."
~ Lieutenant Commander Brent Hodge, US Navy

Where is right thinking applied?

Where do we start with right thinking? It's where we realize that the same principles apply in both the spiritual and the physical realms. For example: right thinking is like the hull of a boat: even if you have it in some places and not in others: your boat won't stay afloat very long!

Philippians 4:8 says "to dwell" which means to focus. 1 John 3: 4-9 says that those who practice righteousness (being right by God's grace and standards) are righteousness and those who don't, are not.

It is this: for what do we hunger and seek? Have you noticed that when people are caught doing something really appalling (chumps), that the follow-up report goes back and shows a pattern of wrongs that trended to this point?

The same with champions: there is a pattern of doing the right things existed that trended to the point of victory. That single fact means that we can take charge and chart our destiny by thinking constantly about our direction, and then *doing* it. Love moves mountains.

Consider healthcare: Kaiser, the Veteran's Administration, Sharp and many others all have an entire department devoted to Mind-Body Medicine, "Complimentary Medicine"/Integrative Medicine (guided imagery, visualization, biofeedback, meditation, etc.). Why? Because where the mind goes, the body starts to follow. They are connected.

The Medical Student Journal of American Medical Association October 4, 2000 p. 1705 study shows huge mind body results:

Fixed on Doing Right

"75% improvement rate in cardiac (heart) complications, 43% bled less in surgery and went home sooner ... cost in hospital savings more than 10 times cost of program."

In *Mind Body Medicine, Evidence-Based Medicine, Clinical Psychophysiology, and Integrative Medicine* from the Association for Applied Psychophysiology and Biofeedback, author Donald Moss, PhD, documents additional better health benefits and savings.

Haven't we all seen examples of right thinking leading to right actions and right results where "attitude determines altitude?" It is the same in all areas of life. I have personally witnessed it in multiple applications: athletics, in any company of believers, as a coach, counselor, personal family, with friends, as a manager, pastor, security organizations, as a team member, and in the company of zealots, or even one zealot. More often than not; the difference is what do we believe? In what do we have faith? How much are we willing to bet on what we believe?

A relatively young person was very concerned and went to the village elder and asked, "You are the wisest, most respected and happiest person I have ever seen. What is your secret to your success? Please share with me. What do I need to do to succeed?"

The elder silently rose and motioned for the seeker to follow. They went to the edge of the water, then went in: over their knees, over their waists, over their shoulders. They walked until the water was over their heads and then walked some more. They stopped and the elder motioned to settle down and wait. So, they waited and waited then the seeker couldn't wait any longer and bolted for the surface but the village elder held the seeker down for a bit more and then finally released.

They got to the shore where the seeker was lying on the ground gasping, and finally shouted, "What was that all about? You nearly drowned me!" The wise one asked, "When you were under the water, what did you want the most? What were you fighting for?" "Air, of course," was the reply. "And you acted as if you believed getting to the surface would solve your situation. Yes?" "Yes, I had to get there." "When you believe about getting it right like you believed about getting air, then you will succeed."

I was in a very young state when I first read books titled **The Magic of Believing**, then **Think and Grow Rich**, and others. I felt it was me against the world; the difference was that I was now convinced it *was* me against the world; yet I realized *they* were outnumbered. Seriously, I knew that there had to be a better way to win and to stay ahead.

Where you start like that, it is amazing how far you can go and what you can do. Then many years later I really read the Bible and found out that once I joined God's team, following His lead (after all, He is the Almighty Creator of the universe), then the world of mere people and their policies were confirmed to be really outnumbered and outgunned because they were going against God!

Holistic is very similar to Whole. For example, the Bible says that we have not because we ask not; also, we have not because we ask for the wrong reason (James 4:2 and 3). Sometimes we get it twisted and think or at least act as if God serves us or answers to us. Crazy, huh?

It helps to read the Biblical Book of Job, especially Chapter 38, and replace Job's name with our names. Now, that is right thinking. In this chapter, Job questions God and God tells Job (you and me): I, God will answer to you when you, a mere mortal, answers me: Where were you when I created the universe? I, God, will be accountable to you when you give account of your actions. Remember that I, God, created life ..." There is a huge and vital difference between asking God to answer us so we can understand His will, versus asking God to answer to us according to our will.

The whole truth is that as we seek what God says and seek to align ourselves to what the Almighty says is right, it is then we can move in faith. Dr. Fred Price wrote a great book whose title sums it up: ***Faith, Foolishness, or Presumption?*** You have got to get the book.

I remember the essence of one part. It is basically that Dr. Price relays that Faith is doing according to what God says; Foolishness is wanting to do, but ignoring what God says.

Presumption is trying to do in spite of what God says. We can get into a lot of trouble by getting a little clip but not bothering to get context. **Stare Decisis** is a legal term meaning the matter has already been decided by a higher authority. No more discussion.

Holistic sometimes means sacrificing what appears certain for what is proven to be sure in spite of what others say. An example is when Peter (a fisherman) stepped out of the boat in the middle of the lake during a storm to walk to Jesus on the water because Jesus told him to "come." Being in the boat (literally, and as an example) is certain; however, trusting the Lord is far surer even if others may not see it that way — yet.

See Matthew 14: 22-33, NIV:

> [22] Immediately Jesus made the disciples get into the boat and go on ahead of him to the other side, while he dismissed the crowd.
> [23] After he had dismissed them, he went up on a mountainside by himself to pray. Later that night, he was there alone, [24] and the boat was already a considerable distance from land, buffeted by the waves because the wind was against it.

Fixed on Doing Right

²⁵ Shortly before dawn Jesus went out to them, walking on the lake. ²⁶ When the disciples saw him walking on the lake, they were terrified. "It's a ghost," they said, and cried out in fear.
²⁷ But Jesus immediately said to them: "Take courage! It is I. Don't be afraid."
²⁸ "Lord, if it's you," Peter replied, "tell me to come to you on the water."
²⁹ "Come," he said.
Then Peter got down out of the boat, walked on the water and came toward Jesus. ³⁰ But when he saw the wind, he was afraid and, beginning to sink, cried out, "Lord, save me!"
³¹ Immediately Jesus reached out his hand and caught him. "You of little faith," he said, "why did you doubt?"
³² And when they climbed into the boat, the wind died down. ³³ Then those who were in the boat worshiped him, saying, "Truly you are the Son of God."

Jesus also compared assurance found only through Him, to finding a great treasure hidden in a field. The person who finds it joyfully sells all their possessions to buy the field to get the prize, even if others may not see it that way — yet.

Here is Matthew: 13 44-46 (NIV):

> **44** "The kingdom of heaven is like treasure hidden in a field. When a man found it, he hid it again, and then in his joy went and sold all he had and bought that field.
> **45** "Again, the kingdom of heaven is like a merchant looking for fine pearls. **46** When he found one of great value, he went away and sold everything he had and bought it."

The movie, **Men of Honor** is based on the real-life experiences of Carl Brashear. Many examples are shown of his choosing to focus on right thinking in spite of incredible spirit-crushing onslaughts.

One inspiring example is that when he lost his leg in heroic service in the Navy, they wanted to give him a medal and a retirement, but he fought back and had them completely cut off his mauled & mangled leg to fit him with a prosthetic so he could finish his career by reaching his goal to be a Navy Master Deep Sea Diver.

Joseph Sadiki shared a revelation about "getting it right: It is a process not just a point." Remember in school when the teacher showed a cutaway of the earth? Layers are present in oil formation. It takes a lot of time, heat, and pressure to transform broken biomass into Black Gold (aka oil).

There are different types of petroleum just like there are different types of people. Please see this website: https://education.nationalgeographic.org/resource/petroleum

Right thinking means studying to know what you are looking at, and looking for. There is the true story shared by Dr. Russell Conwell in his book about a wealthy farmer who heard about others making vast fortunes in the diamond mines on another continent. So, he sold his possessions and traveled there and, unfortunately, went broke. Then he committed suicide, due to not thinking right.

Later the person who bought his farm found a large unusual stone and took it to an expert who told him that it was an uncut diamond. The farm was covered with them and became one of the richest diamond mines of all time. The aptly named book is titled: ***Acres of Diamonds***.
~ https://enjoyingthejourney.org/acres-of-diamonds/

Jesus endured the cross for the joy set before him. (Hebrews 12:2) This is the classic example of right thinking; because even Jesus' closest friends and family failed to understand what was at stake, and that this price He would pay, which was His death, was our salvation plan. Jesus knew that the issue was not price; rather, value. He valued us being restored back to a relationship with God as our Heavenly Father (John 17: 1-3), as priceless and worth any pain, even death on a cross. (Philippians 2: 5-8)

Pastor James Patton

Right thinking is seeing the big picture, not just a single point. Sometimes I stop a presentation and ask a random audience person to just give me $100.00 just because I would like them to. The fun begins listening to all the reasons they would like to but can't. As my mom says, "They have more excuses than Kellogg's has Corn Flakes." Then I say, "What if I told you that I will give the keys and title to my brand-new Mercedes Benz parked outside, because I just got a lawyer's call and my rich uncle whom I didn't know died and left me $1,000,000.00, but I have to be present for the reading of the will in New York tonight with a "price paid" legacy. I need $100.00 to buy the airline ticket in thirty minutes, to go get the money. The first person to give me the $100.00 cash to go get my $1,000,000.00 gets my brand-new car. We will both get a much better return on this exchange.

Everyone always mystically, magically finds a way to get me the money that they didn't have a moment ago. If they don't have it, they tell me that they will call somebody or do something to get it. They plead with me to give them just a moment.

How many of us can relate and would find a way to get the $100.00 for the brand-new Benz? Once we saw the big picture of the prize, the price was painless; it is actually a pleasure to participate, right? That joy is just like a taste of our gift from God.

Fixed on Doing Right

Who needs right thinking?

While right thinking is beneficial to us, it is even more powerful when we infuse others with right thinking. There are countless examples. Some of which that quickly come to mind were made into movies based on true events, such as: ***Coach Carter, Gridiron Gang, Rudy,*** and ***Stand and Deliver***, plus others.

There is a direct correlation between expectations and outcomes regardless of backgrounds.

(*Note*: this does not diminish systemic devastation of past and current social policy injustices; it merely highlights what progress can be accomplished by changing our programming). So, when teenagers were asked, "What is the lowest grade or achievement you can bring home without your parents getting mad at you?" Universally, the truth revealed that the higher the expectation anyone, parents, teachers, coaches, or mentors had for someone, the more that was accomplished.

I remember when I was in Junior High, I really had trouble in math; yet, we had to turn in a huge homework packet each week.

My teacher was understanding of my problems at home and how they hampered me, and was willing to overlook it. Despite my best efforts; my mother and my teacher connected. My mom found out that I was twelve weeks behind. Instantly I was grounded and told that I would engage in no more Judo practice until I was completely caught up for all twelve weeks. It took me ten days.

Phil Crosby tells an account in his book titled **Quality Is Free: The Art of Making Certain** (ISBN 0451622472, 9780451622471) about working as the Quality Control Chief at one of the major aerospace manufactures for the U.S. Department of Defense. One day his boss (the President of the firm) asked him why there were all these variance requests from the contract specifications. "Why couldn't they just do it right with 'Zero Defects' the first time?"

So, Phil explained to him numerous technical reasons that there had to be deviations, and that it was impossible to do it right like it was written. The president thanked Phil for explaining it to him and for all his effort. However, he believed that somewhere in the world there was a Quality Control Chief that could do it right, and he would have liked for that person to have been Phil.

Fixed on Doing Right

Phil wrote that he suddenly had a realization that they were no longer talking about abstracts and deviations. It was not the manufacturing future that was decided. So, Phil went and talked to his Production Chief and explained how they were going to think differently and that the job would be done right the first time: that they were going to focus on that from now on. "Right" meant "Zero Defects."

Well, the Production Chief carefully explained to Phil, with all due respect to their boss, how they couldn't possibly do that. Phil thanked his Production Chief and told him that he believed that somewhere in the world there was a Production Chief who could think right and deliver right the first time and every time, as specified; and Phil really wished that the Production Chief could have been the one.

Phil wrote that he still has the letter from the Department of Defense congratulating them on their unique industry achievement of doing it right the first time, on time, and under budget. When "Zero Defects" is determined not just desired, then "Zero Defects" is delivered.

Proverbs 23:7 says this (Amplified Bible):

"For as he thinks in his heart, so is he ..."

~ Amplified Bible (AMP) Copyright © 2015 by The Lockman Foundation, La Habra, CA 90631. All rights reserved.

What made the Initial *Right Thinking Difference* for Them and Us?

We must see what the real situation is and not be distracted by soundbites and miss where the substantial solutions are. For example: according to U.S. Government National Center for Educational Statistics, May, 2022: "Violent Deaths at School and Away from School Shootings Report" from 07/01/2018 through 06/30/2019: "School-associated violent deaths, (the total of youth deaths), equal thirteen of the 1,508 homicides plus 2,233 youth suicides: 13 of 3,741."

(As an example of how making things right starts with the underlying things, i.e., more safety does not necessarily mean more security, we cite this example regarding planned tragedies.)

Even if we doubled the number of police on a campus, a barricaded shooter would simply shoot the cops first or wait until they were somewhere else.

A police officer with a pistol that maybe has an effective range of 50 yards is not much of an option against a sniper with a rifle with a 600+ yard effective range. At that point all that can be done is to follow practiced safety drills, hide, and call for reinforcements.

Fixed on Doing Right

Prisons have plenty of contraband even though prisoners have been thoroughly strip-searched; so maybe schoolyard methodologies won't work. Achieving safety does not necessarily mean getting more security. Let's get it right.

Maybe we need to use an added security budget to hire more counselors to help map out and mentor positive peer group support (read *Are You Driven To Win? A Roadmap For Young People To Succeed In Life* by Ramona S. Jones), since per FBI 2017 Crime in the United States Report, "40% of all homicides are committed by people who know each other, 10% by strangers, and 50% by someone in an unknown relationship." Where the situation is known, however, that represents 80% of murders. In other words, four of five. Who is connected is a critical key.

For adults, unforgiveness, anger, and stress are known triggers that can lead to numerous serious health problems plus trigger unhealthy coping behaviors that lead to even more physical and psychological health problems.

Please see this website:

https://www.cancer.gov/about-cancer/coping/feelings/stress-fact-sheet

*****

Introducing the Leadership Trilogy:

The applied wisdom of the *Leadership Trilogy* provides you the treasure map, compass, and transport to lift, launch, and most importantly, to leverage way beyond this: up to where you need to be.

This *Leadership Trilogy* of books by Glen Aubrey is designed to be combined, because together they help you and your organization grow in right and profitable ways, building you, your people, and your functional contributions. The goal of each book is to develop maturity on teams who want to work together well, keeping central the fundamental principles that people are more important than production, and relationships come before and give birth to function.

The three components of the trilogy are: *Leadership Is * How To Build Your Legacy, Industrial Strength Solutions * Build Successful Work Teams*, and *Core Teams Work * Their Principles And Practices.* You can leverage these truths to lift and launch you lightyears beyond whatever you felt was your limit. Please access www.creativeteampublishing.com.

Fixed on Doing Right

"The decisions you make today determine your audience tomorrow."
~ Michael Cook

At my church, we have started sending out a daily encouragement scripture with a related word search puzzle and have gotten many positive feedbacks. It is simply an uplifting thought for the day we can grab, on which we can focus, and with which we can move forward.

Sometimes a start of determining a solution means simply stopping in the midst of the stress to remember how much "Amazing Grace" (unmerited favor) and forgiveness we have received from God (sometimes through people), and ask God to let some of the grace we have received flow to us and, more urgently, through us. Some resolution may require us to take more steps to solve the situation. Can a possible side effect of stress related symptoms be solved by doing something to resolve our reaction to an underlying situation? This is part of dwelling right.

An added benefit is that when we talk with each other we have something fresh and positive already built-in that we both start off with. "People over Programs."
~ Glen Aubrey

Daily encouragement positively changes our launch trajectory. We feel energized and elevated afterward. It gets better. There is a peace that passes mere mortal understanding (or no understanding at all) that is based on the grace and favor of the Almighty and Eternal One.

When do we have to think right, so that we can do right?

The key advantage for Christian believers is that when our belief in God is our base, it is the foundation on which everything is built. The Bible compares it to a house built on a foundation of solid rock and when (not if) the storms of life come, the house withstands the onslaught. (Matthew 17:24-29)

Without that relationship being anchored on the written unchanging word of God, we are just holding on to sand which can quickly wash away and everything will crumble with catastrophic loss. There is a reason that building codes exist, along with product safety specifications, and rules of the road.

Natural laws like gravity exist as well.

Fixed on Doing Right

What if, when someone honestly believes that he or she can defy gravity and physics, just jumps off a 40-story building? What do you think will be the outcome then? The Bible says to consider the outcome of people's faith in God, and dwell on doing right (Hebrews Chapter 11, and Hebrews 13:7).

Consider these Bible characters as examples: Abigail, Daniel, David, Deborah, Esther, Gideon, Joseph, Mary, Moses, Paul, Peter, Ruth, and Sarah... Like us, they were not perfect. The direction on which they dwelled determined their destination and destiny like it will determine ours.

We must constantly think about what is right so when the key moment arrives and others need us, it will be our practiced reflex to avoid:

1. "First, they came for the Socialists, and I did not speak out—because I was not a Socialist.
2. Then they came for the Trade Unionists, and I did not speak out—because I was not a Trade Unionist.
3. Then they came for the Jews, and I did not speak out—because I was not a Jew.
4. Then they came for me—and there was no one left to speak for me."
    ~ Pastor Martin Niemöller, Nazi Sympathizer, Opposition Leader, Prisoner, and more.

"Those who fail to learn from history are doomed to repeat it".
~ Winston Churchill

"Never Again"
~ Meir Kahane

Right thinking means that we must recognize and repent (turn away from) past wrongs. "The condition upon which God hath given liberty to man is eternal vigilance; which condition if he break, servitude is at once the consequence of his crime and the punishment of his guilt."
~ John Philpot Curran (repeated by Thomas Jefferson, Fredrick Douglas and others, per Monticello.Org).

We must be on guard against those who would soft sell or downplay danger to us in order to lull us into a false sense of security, just to be ambushed again. We must be like the people of Berea who examined carefully what was said to see if it was true (Acts 17:11).

We must move based on what is right to restore balance. Objective truth is the standard, not self-serving Historical Negationism sympathizers. "Historical Negationism refers to the refusal to accept an historical event, such as the Holocaust ..."
~ Please see: Vocabulary—Texas Holocaust and Genocide Commission https://thgc.texas.gov vocabulary

Fixed on Doing Right

"Right is remembering F.A.M.I.LY. F̲orget A̲bout M̲e. I̲ L̲ove Y̲ou."
~ Chaplain Mickey Stonier, PhD.

No sane person would agree to "stay still 'just for now,'" and keep playing against a stacked deck and not want it checked and corrected (made right), especially if the more it was checked, the more cheating was found. That is akin to an embezzler saying, "The problem is that there is an audit." Tacit consent is guilt (accessory or accomplice crimes).

Let's not excuse ourselves by saying, "Look, we didn't know."

For God understands all hearts, and He sees yours and mine. He who guards our souls already knows what we knew.

See Proverbs 24: 12 (NIV):

> [12] If you say, "But we knew nothing about this," does not he who weighs the heart perceive it? Does not he who guards your life know it? Will he not repay everyone according to what they have done?

God holds us all accountable when we choose to not acknowledge wrongs, and to ignore what is right.

Pastor James Patton

Note this scripture regarding "The Final Judgment" in Matthew 25:31-46 (NIV):

> 31 "When the Son of Man comes in his glory, and all the angels with him, then he will sit upon his glorious throne. 32 All the nations will be gathered in his presence, and he will separate the people as a shepherd separates the sheep from the goats. 33 He will place the sheep at his right hand and the goats at his left.
>
> 34 "Then the King will say to those on his right, 'Come, you who are blessed by my Father, inherit the Kingdom prepared for you from the creation of the world. 35 For I was hungry, and you fed me. I was thirsty, and you gave me a drink. I was a stranger, and you invited me into your home. 36 I was naked, and you gave me clothing. I was sick, and you cared for me. I was in prison, and you visited me.'
>
> 37 "Then these righteous ones will reply, 'Lord, when did we ever see you hungry and feed you? Or thirsty and give you something to drink? 38 Or a stranger and show you hospitality? Or naked and give you clothing? 39 When did we ever see you sick or in prison and visit you?' 40 "And the King will say, 'I tell you the truth, when you did it to one of the least

Fixed on Doing Right

of these my brothers and sisters, you were doing it to me!'

⁴¹ "Then the King will turn to those on the left and say, 'Away with you, you cursed ones, into the eternal fire prepared for the devil and his demons. ⁴² For I was hungry, and you didn't feed me. I was thirsty, and you didn't give me a drink. ⁴³ I was a stranger, and you didn't invite me into your home. I was naked, and you didn't give me clothing. I was sick and in prison, and you didn't visit me.' ⁴⁴ "Then they will reply, 'Lord, when did we ever see you hungry or thirsty or a stranger or naked or sick or in prison, and not help you?'

⁴⁵ "And he will answer, 'I tell you the truth, when you refused to help the least of these my brothers and sisters, you were refusing to help me.' ⁴⁶ "And they will go away into eternal punishment, but the righteous will go into eternal life."

We are to actively seek justice: not just joyride.

Isaiah 59:14-19 (New Living Translation, NLT) relates that God was amazed that no one helped the oppressed (did what was right by helping others). Here is the context:

"¹⁴ Our courts oppose the righteous, and justice is nowhere to be found. Truth stumbles in the streets, and honesty has been outlawed. ¹⁵ Yes, truth is gone, and anyone who renounces evil is attacked. The LORD looked and was displeased to find there was no justice. ¹⁶ He was amazed to see that no one intervened to help the oppressed. So he himself stepped in to save them with his strong arm, and his justice sustained him. ¹⁷ He put on righteousness as his body armor and placed the helmet of salvation on his head. He clothed himself with a robe of vengeance and wrapped himself in a cloak of divine passion. ¹⁸ He will repay his enemies for their evil deeds. His fury will fall on his foes. He will pay them back even to the ends of the earth. ¹⁹ In the west, people will respect the name of the LORD; in the east, they will glorify him. For he will come like a raging flood tide driven by the breath of the LORD."

~ *Holy Bible*, New Living Translation, copyright © 1996, 2004, 2015 by Tyndale House Foundation. Used by permission of Tyndale House Publishers, Inc., Carol Stream, Illinois 60188. All rights reserved.

Note that God tells us to put on His armor in Ephesians 6:10-18 for the purpose being equipped for doing what is right. Equality is not equity if it reinforces a wrong.

Fixed on Doing Right

What if a football team was caught distracting or bribing the referees and, as a result, the cheating team had twice as many players on the field as they were supposed to have (22 vs. 11)? And they say: "This has always been that way." Then they offer, "Let's just leave it that way and, by the way, don't check the game films because we have been doing this for a long time and have a winning record. Let's just play on like it is: you, the victim doesn't get to even the field by adding equity players. Cheaters keep cheating plus keep their lopsided benefits and, by the way, let's celebrate the scoundrels: just get over it." Note: Olympics retracts medals.

Then the victims are labeled as "losers" to add insult to injury. Instead: let's check the stats and see if they are skewed and screwed; then <u>respond by doing what is right: just like we would want it done for us now and always</u>.

Please see Matthew 22:37-40 (NIV). It concludes with this command:

"Love your neighbor as yourself."

If your family unfortunately included the notorious rapist Jack the Ripper, would you brag about it? Would you ever build a statue honoring Hitler? We can't enjoy the benefits and ignore the blame, or we become part of the problem: that is why we boycott "Blood Diamonds" and other "Blood Money." Because right is right.

It's not necessarily convenient. We have the power to be honest and render honor to those whom honor is due and, as a matter of honor, discipline those deserving of it.

> "If not us, then who?
> If not now, then when?"

~ John E. Lewis, U.S. House Of Representatives (1987-2020)
tags: action, change, civil-rights, integrity, moral-courage, personal-responsibility
https://www.goodreads.com/quotes/193401-if-not-us-then-who-if-not-now-then-when

Where else do we have to be right?

How about in what we do, think, and what we say? The Bible states, and surely experience shows, that out of the abundance of the heart the mouth speaks. Please see Matthew 12: 24.

Please observe James 3:3-6:

> "³ When we bridle horses and put bits in their mouths to lead them wherever we want, we can control their whole bodies. ⁴ Consider ships: They are so large that strong winds are needed to drive them. But pilots direct their ships wherever they want with a little rudder. ⁵ In the same way, even though the tongue is a small part of the body, it boasts wildly. Think about

this: A small flame can set a whole forest on fire. ⁶ The tongue is a small flame of fire ... "

Life and death are in the power of the tongue, according to Proverbs 18:21.

Observe Matthew 15:18:

> "But what comes out of the mouth proceeds from the heart and defiles a person."

For example: where does it leave us when we downplay and describe mass murder genocide in an effort to annihilate and eliminate an entire group of people as "ethnic cleansing," or use our "right of freedom of speech" or the right of "freedom of religion" to incite some to enslave or endanger others? Where is this "right" there?

Dwelling on right means destroying the deadly disease of Doublespeak.

Definition of "Doublespeak: dŭb'əl-spēk" <u>noun</u>

~ From the American Heritage® Dictionary of the English Language, 5th Edition.

1. "Any language deliberately constructed to disguise or distort its actual meaning, often by employing euphemism or ambiguity. Typically used by governments or large institutions.

2. Any language that pretends to communicate but actually does not."

For example, consider calling or teaching "Genocide" as "Ethnic Cleaning."

The actual definition according to the Convention on the Prevention and Punishment of the Crime of Genocide Article II is this:

"In the present Convention, genocide means any of the following acts committed with intent to destroy, in whole or in part, a national, ethnical, racial or religious group, as such:

1. Killing members of the group;
2. Causing serious bodily or mental harm to members of the group;
3. Deliberately inflicting on the group conditions of life calculated to bring about its physical destruction in whole or in part;
4. Imposing measures intended to prevent births within the group;
5. Forcibly transferring children of the group to another group."

~ https://www.un.org/en/genocideprevention/genocide.shtml
United Nations Office On Genocide Prevention And The Responsibility To Protect

Fixed on Doing Right

Other examples of Doublespeak include:

1. "Premeditated Murder of An Innocent Baby In the Womb" as "Women's Right to Choose"
2. "Wife Beating" / "Assault Likely to Cause Great Bodily Harm" as "Domestic Dispute"/ "Discipline"
3. "Slavery" as "Human Trafficking"
4. "Fraud" as "Alternative Facts"

Doublespeak is doubly deadly because of the victims it lists, plus those who become victims by listening and being led to do wrong by not dwelling on what is truly right.

It is not about "Political Correctness." <u>It is vitally about what is "Morally and Factually Right."</u>

In our hearts, we must do better than that to start. Right?

Where else do we want to be secure and successful? The Bible uses the example of sheep following The Good Shepherd who will lay down His life to keep them safe and satisfied. (John 10:11-18) This is His answer, always.

You see, our enemy is always lurking in the shadows — on the edge, trying to lure us off to be ambushed (1 Peter 5:8). This is especially true in the middle of life's storms of chaos and clutter.

We must actively listen for the calm still voice of the One who loves us, like a child who listens and looks for his or her loving parent. The Good Shepherd uses His staff and rod to gently guide us, and to reach out and rescue us when needed, even if we're not listening. That is His comfort. (Psalm 23:4)

Thinking of ourselves as sheep or children who need to listen and learn is not hard when we consider not *who* we are: but *whose* we are. It is an honor being blessed by the grace (unmerited favor) of Almighty God, Creator of the Universe, the all-knowing owner of all.

<u>Summary:</u>

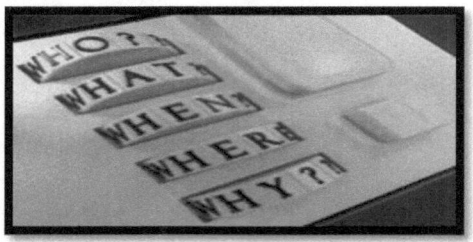

1. What is right?
   "What is just, good, or proper; conforming to facts."
2. Why dwell on what is right? "Dwelling on, prevents deviance from."
3. Who decides what is right? "Right is decided by God, who is ***the*** authority."
4. When do we need to dwell on right? "When we want it for us." (This is "right now!" and "all the time.")
5. Where do we dwell on right? "Literally everywhere."

Fixed on Doing Right

The reality is this: we think right, we dwell right, we do right, and end up right. We don't have to settle for less.

Romans 12:2 (CEB):

> "Don't be conformed to the pattern of this world but be transformed by the renewing of our mind then you will be able to test and approve what God's will is—His good, pleasing and perfect will."
> ~ Common English Bible (CEB) Copyright © 2011 by Common English Bible

Thanks for giving us the opportunity to state what was given and shared with us, and works for us, and hopefully will help work for you, too. Think, dwell on, and do right.

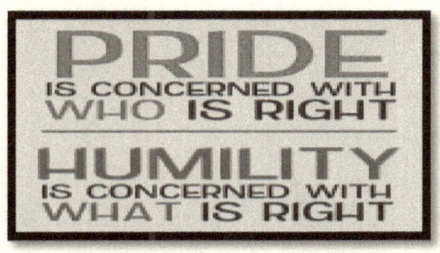

Warmest regards, Pastor James Patton
T.E.A.M. (Together Everyone Achieves More)
July-August, 2022

*****

Pastor James Patton

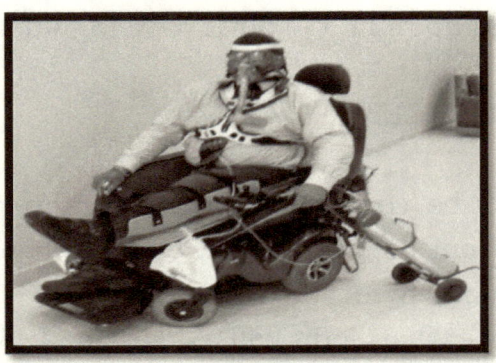

Pastor James Patton, July-August, 2022

ART CREDIT: All Art / Graphic Illustrations for this chapter (except the James Patton photo) are of part of the www.Dreamstime.com collection and are used by licensed permission.

Fixed on Doing Right

From James: How I met and associated with Glen Aubrey:

I had the pleasure of meeting my beloved brother, Glen Aubrey, decades ago when we were both at San Diego Youth for Christ. Glen was on the Executive Team staff and I was a part-time volunteer. Glen was always so upbeat and on fire for excellence and vision that he was like a gust of fresh air whenever he came in. Glen made time to inquire about families, people, their goals, and gifts. Glen has a truly unique gift of passion for spirit—led excellence. He lives and breathes his mantra: "People are more important than projects or programs."

When I first met Glen, he was in charge of Development (raising the big bucks needed for a major ministry), then he led the Y2 program which was a contemporary outreach for Adults (Youth for Christ was only reaching part of the family at this time).

This was truly amazing because these are three totally different paradigms (numbers planning, spiritual leadership, and raw, creative talent). It is like the three parts of our processing (logic, will, and emotion) that are often oppositional when operating at high levels. We tend to focus on one. Glen glides between each and, with all three, gracefully uplifts the others.

Later I had the honor, privilege, and joy of watching Glen work with organizations both in the commercial and church world.

Like a Maestro: Glen is an orchestra conductor, director, and producer all rolled into one. Typically, an organization engaged many talented specialists people. Glen gets them to all play the same music together where each is showcased and, meanwhile all are supportive to the whole synergy. For example, he worked with a church and invites the Pastor/Leader to seek God months in advance enabling them as a catalyst, to write out a schedule of the message and illustrations. All team members communicate, coordinate, and commit in writing down to the very second what every element is doing and why they are doing it.

Every joint (part) combines to convey the plan of God. The result is transforming. Everyone grows professionally, spiritually, and relationally. This growth happens in all environments in which Glen was involved.

Glen's love for God and people brings out God's best in those people involved. Glen has inspired, encouraged, and blessed me far beyond belief. As a matter of fact, you are not reading what I wrote alone; you are being blessed by what our team scribbled and drooled at Glen's urging. Then Glen graciously rewrote it.

As we were preparing this chapter, we were reminded of the story of a huge formal concert hall with a single grand piano onstage for the master to play. Suddenly the curtain opens and to the parents' horror, their small child was sitting there trying to pound out "Twinkle, Twinkle, Little Star." The famous pianist comes up behind him and whispers "keep playing" while he reaches around on both sides and overlays and incorporates a masterpiece.

The message is: "Encouragement, Pass It On."
~ https://www.youtube.com/watch?v=-JWh0ZWmFWw

Were it not for Glen's ghostwriting and assistance with my ministry and me personally, we would not be writing here. The transforming love and grace of God constantly and consistently is demonstrated through Glen Aubrey. We highly recommend that you visit this website:

www.creativeteampublishing.com

You will be blessed beyond belief.

Glen's books and teachings have blessed and continue to transform us. Thank you, Glen, very much.

From Glen: How I met James Patton:

It was when James and I were laboring for the Lord in San Diego Youth for Christ (YFC) in the late 1980s that we formed a life-long friendship. This friendship has deepened through the years. I highly respect James as a caring minister of the Gospel of Christ. His comments in this chapter are, in a word, "Right!"

Chapter Four
Pure

By Glen Aubrey

Many scriptures resonated with me in college. One was this:

James 1:27 (NIV):

> "Religion that God our Father accepts as **pure and faultless** is this: to look after orphans and widows in their distress and to keep oneself from being polluted by the world."

When you and I desire to live righteously, we best demonstrate our desires to follow God as we care for others. Through these actions, we can become more like Christ, which is our ultimate desire. Indeed, in our actions we can become Christ's hands and feet for those in need. This action requires going to them and offering time, treasure, truth, and resources to them.

I vividly remember utilizing this scripture in an answer to a question of belief and practicing faith, in a college Pastoral Theology class. To the professor, it was insufficient and, as politely as I could, I disagreed.

After all, the book of James is part of canonized scripture. In my opinion, this passage carries much weight. The professor and I chose to agree to disagree. No problem.

The perception of a lack of acceptance lingers, however; not of my answer; rather, in the refusal of the professor to accept what I considered then and now to be deeper truths.

The context which this scripture verse concludes, paints graphic illustrations of what I term "faith lacking in understanding, and insufficient or disobedient action, sharply contrasted with righteous living." The passage dealt with problems like these: anger, the degradation of moral filth, and James' admonition to humbly accept the word, "which can save you." Prior to this, James instructs the brothers and sisters to "not be deceived," declaring every perfect gift is from above, offered to us from a God who doesn't change, like "shifting shadows." He accents the "word of truth" so the believers would become what he terms "first fruits" (evidences) of all God created.

I see that as joyful responsibility with positive, eternal consequences.

Whatever Is Pure

Further, the reference above followed instructions to persevere in trials, the heavenly reward for doing so, the struggle with temptation, that temptation is not from God; James telling us what temptation really is: "[14] but each person is tempted when they are dragged away by their own evil desire and enticed. [15] Then, after desire has conceived, it gives birth to sin; and sin, when it is full-grown, gives birth to death."

James blatantly issues a warning for us is to not be deceived.

Practical admonitions like these begin in verse 19 of James 1: "[19] ... Everyone should be quick to listen, slow to speak and slow to become angry, [20] because human anger does not produce the righteousness that God desires."

In verse 25: "[25] But whoever looks intently into the perfect law that gives freedom – not forgetting what they have heard, but doing it – they will be blessed in what they do." He adds to those instructions a warning about controlling conversations: "[26] Those who consider themselves religious and yet do not keep a tight rein on their tongues deceive themselves, and their religion is worthless."

"Worthless" is a strong term.

The context points to, what is in my mind, a God-birthed conclusion found in the verse that started this chapter,

James 1:27. Let's inquire: what is "pure and faultless" religion or a series of relational beliefs that our God accepts? In my reading it is to help others, meeting material and more to those who need assistance in distress and "to keep oneself from being polluted by the world."

A practical and lasting truth appears to be this: you and I are in charge of what we believe and how we act. The admonition from James is for us to **_do_ faith not just declare it.** *We* become God's hands and feet of help to those in need, showing our faith *by* our deeds. *We* become the individuals through whom God's work in the world is evidenced in our lives. A watching and needful world awaits. Further, they so often need what you and I can provide.

> … you and I are in charge of what we believe and how we act. The admonition from James is for us to **_do_ faith, not just declare it.**

*****

Close to that same time, as a collegian, I composed this song: **Never Will God Leave You Comfortless.** It is © 1972 by Glen Aubrey. All Rights Reserved.

I was living in Pasadena at the time not far from Vernon Lintvedt, my dear friend from San Diego. In fact, he resided just up the street. I shared this song with him.

Whatever Is Pure

    I invite you to sing it if you like (the music follows); for sure, review the lyrics, and see how it may touch you in ways like it touched me. The admonition is this: we endeavor to encourage others and help them in their tests, trials, temptations, and struggles, assuring them that God can meet their needs. The beauty of this is that many of those needs are fulfilled by us.

    A scan of the original music from 1972, follows the lyrics.

<u>Lyrics</u>:

Never will God leave you comfortless,
Through ev'ry trial He will be by your side.
His strength will be your stay ev'ry moment of each day,
He will always be your Friend and your Guide.

When life is filled with problems,
And the pressures mount up so tall;
You don't know if you're gonna make it,
You feel like you're gonna fall.

Remember that God is with you,
So when the times get rough,
To know He cares and loves you,
Well, that's enough!

Remember that God is with you,
So when the times get rough,

Glen Aubrey

To know He cares and loves you,
Well, that's enough!

*****

Remember: <u>God cares and loves others *through* us,
His children</u>.

*****

Never Will God Leave You Comfortless

Never Will God Leave You Comfortless

Never Will God Leave You Comfortless

Never Will God Leave You Comfortless

Never Will God Leave You Comfortless

Never Will God Leave You Comfortless

Never Will God Leave You Comfortless

Never Will God Leave You Comfortless

Never Will God Leave You Comfortless

We seek, or should earnestly look, for ways to touch others at the point of their needs, while seeking to honor God, giving Him the credit and the praise. The methods vary, surely. Often, I have found that God reveals His will and design for us to touch others with meaningful words and tasks for His glory. The benefits are never one-dimensional: they are for our good even as they benefit those we reach.

As a musician, I am fond of sharing my gifts with those God may send my way. Often, I seek these opportunities. The music shared, while apparently appreciated by the listeners, may through the guidance of God touch the hearers with truth. That offering is a unique and special privilege.

What gifts can you offer to others in your desire to be a practitioner of God's pure and faultless religion? Let me recommend this action: make a list of your potential offerings and those to whom these offerings can be presented in the right time and place. Probably nothing is more soul satisfying than active service when the goal is to give and not care who gets the credit, as long as God is glorified.

In the process, accept with gratitude any thanks offered for your gift, and then (a practice I have shared for years), thank them for what they (the recipients) mean to you. Affirm **them**.

Whatever Is Pure

Always point your "audience" (those who receive from you) to God as the Source of all good gifts. It is mutually beneficial.

I am not surprised at how God ministers through us to others if and when we make ourselves available to follow His leading. Let's ask ourselves, "Is our practice of relational religion 'pure and faultless' before the Lord?" I sincerely hope so. Here's an admonition: strive to give thanks to God for each day of blessing He grants to us so we are blessed as we share with other people.

*****

Chapter Five
Lovely

The Eyes Have It
By Glen Aubrey

When I am in a grocery store to do weekly shopping (and most of us visit stores like this frequently), I look for a "believer's eyes" in the countenance of someone I have not met yet, a perfect stranger. In my experience when I see a fellow-shopper and I learn that he or she is a believer, referring to their visible and viable faith, I turn to them and say, "I could see it in your eyes." It's true.

Eyes are instruments God gave us to not only view our worlds, but to be testimonies of light and faith, as well. The eyes of a believer are what I call "lovely:" uplifting, beautiful, transparent, inviting, warm, and friendly.

Eyes of a declared unbeliever often cannot be described as such; rather, they may appear dark, subdued, sad, forlorn, and in some cases, even menacing.

How often have you witnessed these differences?

Recently, again while picking up a few necessities at a local market, I saw a 40-year-old body builder. I mean, he was *built*! Nice guy, too. After I greeted him, I mentioned the obvious, and he said he had a gym at home. Interestingly, for as big and built as he was, he told me he ate seven small meals a day (each one the size of a man's hand), and was deeply dedicated to health and well-being. He was pleasant, engaging, and accepting.

His eyes told me he was a Christian, so I asked him, just to confirm my suspicion. His resounding "yes" was power-packed with compassion and truth. I told him that I "could see it in his eyes." His relationship with Christ was obvious, compelling, friendly, and true.

In the DVD *Chosen* series (currently seasons one and two are released with more seasons to come), an actress portrays the role of Mary Magdalene. Of course, we have no idea what she really looked like; there were no cameras back in that day! However, the actress portraying Mary possessed a lovely countenance, smile, and warm, gentle eyes. She personified and expressed hope, humility, peace, gratitude, and love.

Those positive traits had not always been a part of her life. In her former life, she was not one who followed God. Her eyes at that time, were not lovely; she was not in a right alignment with God. In fact, she was far from Him. In that state, she was lost and undone, "without God and His Son."

Whatever Is Lovely

Although this event is not actually recorded in scripture, we are shown in the series how Jesus recognized her pain and lovingly confronted her with compassion. He reached to her in her fallen state and called her by name. He gently said to her, "You are Mine."

Mary experienced the overwhelming love from the Son of God, and was redeemed. His touch, and her acceptance of His grace and mercy, changed her.

Her whole countenance, including her eyes, became lovely. This was transformation from the inside out. Can you and I even imagine this change in someone, which occurred over 2,000 years ago? Well, it's true. God's transformation doesn't just affect the soul; it changes all of a person, including their countenance.

I ran into a fairly elderly teacher, in her late 80s, whose eyes spoke of gratitude, redemption, and undying love. Upon my inquiry, she joyfully admitted her Christ-like faith, stating how much she had enjoyed teaching. The thought struck me: she was still enjoying it: *she was teaching me!* How I enjoyed this interaction!

Lovely faith is contagious faith. It's real. It's attractive.

| Lovely faith is contagious faith. It's real. It's attractive. |

Why is "lovely" a part of this list composed by the Apostle Paul? It may have nothing to do with physical attractiveness, at least on the surface; it does have everything to do with a cleansed spirit, one that is born again, and in right standing with God. This is renewal from the inside out.

> This is renewal from the inside out.

When I was very young, my family went "cat shopping." My parents had agreed to purchase a Siamese feline for me as a pet, to enjoy and purposely teach me ownership and responsibility. This was the second time. The first Siamese cat we had owned had disappeared after many years. We were searching for a replacement.

As I recall, the first acquisition was thrilling for this young boy. The second: not so much.

The man who sold us the second cat had mistrusting, foreboding eyes. They spoke of shadiness, and taking advantage of his customers.

Why was this evident? The answer is simple: regardless of the age of the customers, "I could see it in his eyes."

My encouragement to you, if you are follower of Christ, is to let your eyes show it! The eyes have it!

Whatever Is Lovely

Remember when our Lord spoke of lighting a lamp? Here's the account:

Matthew 5:15 (NIV):

> Neither do people light a lamp and put it under a bowl. Instead they put it on its stand, and it gives light to everyone in the house.

Our eyes are more than just physical gifts (a "sensory structure which is light-sensitive" according to Merriam-Webster) with which to see and observe. I have discovered they can also be "lights" in a darkened world, to touch everyone we see. Let's be sure nothing dims our lights!

My good friend, Jim Robeson, who also has a chapter in this book (Chapter 8 on Praiseworthy), reminded me of this scripture which further underscores the importance of the "eye" as the lamp of the body.

Here are the verses in Matthew 6:22 and 23 (NIV):

> [22] The eye is the lamp of the body. If your eyes are healthy, your whole body will be full of light. [23] But if your eyes are unhealthy, your whole body will be full of darkness. If then the light within you is darkness, how great is that darkness!

How powerful is a small light in someone's eyes, a darkened room, or even a sports stadium?

In 1972, an event occurred which literally changed the world. It was a significant part of what became known as the "Jesus Revolution." At the Cotton Bowl in Dallas, Texas, Reverend Dr. Billy Graham, along with Dr. Bill Bright of Campus Crusade for Christ, hosted an event for some 100,000 people. Although I was not physically present (I just had graduated from high school and was entering college in Southern California), *everyone* heard about this crusade and relished the effects of this new "Jesus Revolution."

Those effects are still felt today, as they should be. Nothing can stop the light of God's truth.

Please see:
~https://www.google.com/search?q=Jesus+Revolution+1972&tbm=isch&hl=en&sa=X&ved=2ahUKEwiyoLGcl7_3AhUBUM0KHe27DL8Q3VYoAHoECAEQHg&biw=1465&bih=718#imgrc=jwwLsS8g_jNUrM

And you are invited to visit this reference:
~https://www.youtube.com/watch?v=DOVjLF7bNac

In the course of the crusade, Dr. Graham, on the night of June 15, 1972, asked that the lights of the stadium be turned out. In that moment, in a completely darkened stadium, he lit one candle, and passed the flame along to another person with a candle. This spreading light continued until a hundred thousand candles were burning all at once in the stadium. It was quite a sight!

> Please see this site, or just Google Cotton Bowl Candle Lighting, June 15, 1972:
>
> ~https://www.google.com/search?q=cotton+bowl+candle+lighting&source=hp&ei=aP9uYpXHBt290PEPn76OiA8&iflsig=AJiK0e8AAAAAYm8NeAaaIXYR3LtXuCpQnrzYFj8Y3ZbC&ved=0ahUKEwiVm8mFo7_3AhXdHjQIHR-fA_EQ4dUDCAk&uact=5&oq=cotton+bowl+candle+lighting&gs_lcp=Cgdnd3Mtd2l6EAM6BQgAEIAEOgsILhCABBDHARCjAjoLCC4QgAQQxwEQ0QM6CAguEIAEENQCOggIABCABBDJAzoFCAAQkgM6CwguEIAEEMcBEK8BOgUILhCABDoOCC4QgAQQxwEQrwEQ1AJQAFj3dWCyfWgAcAB4AIABuwGIAbMWkgEFMTUuMTKYAQCgAQE&sclient=gws-wiz

This 100,000 candle light demonstration became literally an illustration of "One Way," demonstrating that Jesus was and is the only way to God. "One Way" was graphically illustrated by the index finger of one hand being raised.

> Please see:
> ~https://sdebeaubien.wordpress.com/2021/07/10/the-jesus-people-movement/

The public event was international in scope, showing true redemption and reconciliation to God through Christ's love and forgiveness, an outpouring of God's immeasurable grace.

In 2022, 50 years later, the Cotton Bowl hosts another eventl, June 24th and 25th. See this website:

https://together22.pulse.org/home/

The intent, focus, and plan of this event is a relevant, contemporary, and contagious demonstration of the love of Christ, inviting all who hear and experience this, to come to know Him personally.

So, let us consider this question once more: how important is the light of God's presence, beginning in your eyes, invading and flooding your life, reaching your networks, as well as friends and family?

The lovely and loving light of God shines to reach the world. Let *your* light shine!

Actually, allowing the light of truth and love to shine, is a command:

Whatever Is Lovely

Matthew 5:16 (NIV):

> In the same way, let your light shine before others, that they may see your good deeds and glorify your Father in heaven.

The results of "this little light of mine" are far reaching, eternal in scope, and life-changing in results!

Remember this song for kids?

> This little light of mine, I'm gonna let it shine
> This little light of mine, I'm gonna let it shine
> This little light of mine, I'm gonna let it shine
> Let it shine, let it shine, let it shine
>
> Jesus is the Light, and I'm gonna let Him shine
> Jesus is the Light, I'm gonna let Him shine
> Jesus is the Light, and I'm gonna let Him shine
> Let Him shine, let Him shine, let Him shine
>
> Let it shine, let it shine, let it shine
> Let it shine, let it shine, let it shine
>
> ~ Source: Musixmatch

Where did the song originate? According to Wikipedia:

"The origin of the song is unclear, but the phrase 'This little light of mine' appears published in poetry in 1925 by Edward G. Ivins, a writer in Montana."

Regardless of origin, that truth and desire to let our lights shine, rings true today, and always will.

To close this chapter: my family and I were privileged to present music and programming arts ministry at Forest Home Christian Conference Center, located in Forest Falls, California, during the 1980s and 1990s. Up in those San Bernardino mountains rising above Redlands and Yucaipa, very little city light covered up the splendor of a starlit sky.

Shining stars composed spectacular displays of God's magnificence. The unending expanse of His creation was easy to find: just look up at night. Following the North Star, and locating constellations became a pleasant evening pastime. The Big Dipper, Little Dipper, and other constellations were clearly visible.

How far away are those stars that make up many of the constellations we can see on a clear night? According to Google, referenced in January 28, 2021: "The distance from Earth to the closest star in the Big Dipper, Megrez, is 340,000,000,000,000 miles." Yet, even at that distance, the stars of the constellation were bright with light, ever there, always shining.

Most people recognize and know about the North Star. According to Google, 2019 and 2022: "The North Star or Pole Star—aka Polaris—is famous for holding nearly still in our sky while the entire northern sky moves around it. That's because it's located nearly at the north celestial pole, the point around which the entire northern sky turns. Polaris marks the way "due north."

The distance from earth to the North Star is about 323 light-years. Just to remind us all, a light year is a unit of astronomical distance equivalent to the distance that light travels in one year, which is 9.4607×10^{12} km (nearly 6 trillion miles).

We can enjoy the light though trillions of miles away! Such is the power of light in the darkness of space.

The starry sky is awesome to view on a clear night. Its beauty is lovely beyond comprehension. Did the Apostle Paul have that thought in mind when he penned "lovely?" Perhaps we will never know this side of eternity.

But in my mind, the bridge from "lovely to light" makes "lovely" take on a whole new and dramatic meaning.

Again, let *your* light shine!

Chapter Six
Admirable

By Glen Aubrey

Admirable: To be admired; worthy of admiration; having qualities to excite wonder, with approbation, esteem or reverence.

How can God's intimate relationship with each of us be described any loftier and purer than this? This description is on a level all its own. It is "high and lifted up."

Note this passage in Isaiah 6:1 (KJV):

> [1] In the year that king Uzziah died I saw also the LORD sitting upon a throne, high and lifted up, and his train filled the temple.

A king of Judah had passed away. In that time of death, sorrow, and sadness at a loss of life, the living God revealed Himself as living and Holy to His prophet. Isaiah recorded this incident for us. At this time, the prophet declared, "I also saw the Lord." God's exaltation became evident in a time of loss.

How true is this juxtaposition of God's life and human loss or struggle whenever it's needed the most?

In times of loss, God's presence and goodness transcend and surpass human events no matter what they are—even death.

God's involvement is set apart; described often as "holy." What a polar contrast with familiar, human, common, and earthly circumstances!

"Holy" means Properly, whole, entire or perfect, in a moral sense. Hence, pure in heart, temper or dispositions; free from sin and sinful affections. ~ Merriam-Webster 1828 [Note: Webster's definitions 2022 have changed since this classic version.]

We are given to understand that "Admirable" is beyond our experience, yet we must "think" on it, and in those thoughts, let God have His ways within us to mold us into His likeness. Although this quality trait of God's indwelling is greater than we ever could imagine, the implication is that we can enjoy it as we become more like Christ.

I was reminded of the true story of a little boy, age five, who was called of God to pray for his father, that his dad would become a believer in Christ. So, each Sunday in church, for five years, the boy obeyed. God answered his prayers in the little boy's tenth year. The change was miraculous, wondrous, remarkable, holy, and yes, admirable. It was deserving of the highest esteem. I know in both the dad and boy's lives this occurrence was more than surprising; yet, it was gratefully embraced.

How does God "surprise" you? When I was a sophomore at Pasadena College, Pasadena, California, I had little money; most college students can identify with that condition! God's involvement in my life at that time became remarkable.

I had not been renting a room off campus for very long when in the mail, an envelope arrived with no return address. The handwriting was a little bit scribbled and addressed to me. The cursive lettering was not recognizable (though today and for many years I believe I knew who sent the communication; however, I have never asked). In the envelope was one $20.00 bill: which equated to just enough to sustain me for another month. Further, the money flowed every month for the whole time I was living there and in school. When after a year I changed colleges, the cash money payments of $20.00 per month ceased.

The ongoing gift for a year was surprising, for sure. I did not need to know who sent it, though I wondered. With an attitude of gratitude, I simply accepted it.

Often God's provision is just like that. Our response may not need to be a full knowledge of who or why; rather, just submissive acceptance in thanksgiving at His provision.

Throughout my life God's provision became one of many surprises. "Surprises" by definition are never planned or known in advance; otherwise, the term "surprise" would not apply.

Was receiving tangible funds admirable, allowed by God, and did that gift increase personal faith in Him, to supply and sustain me through no planning or involvement of my own? Undoubtedly, yes.

"Admirable" became a hallmark of God's involvement with me. In his Philippians list composed by the Apostle Paul, we see that Admirable is one of God's character traits used to describe His design of a lifestyle often of wonder for believers to embrace. It is to be considered in thought, internalized in meditation, and incorporated into daily activity.

Let's look at the life of Christ. What about the life and ministry of Jesus could be described as "admirable?" One event stands out perhaps surpassing all others, a central anchor upon which our faith rests. I am referring to the Resurrection.

Everyone living dies eventually, of course; death appears to be a part of life, simply because it is. Only One Life lived again *after* death. Jesus' death and Resurrection was predicted in the passage of Psalm 22 among many other scriptures. This Psalm was written a multitude of years earlier than the actual events. These events were more than a little surprising to

Admirable

Christ's followers at that time. In fact, more than 500 followers simultaneously witnessed the resurrected Christ. (1 Corinthians 15:6). The proofs are undeniable, sustainable, and compose a graphic example of verifiable truth.

The Resurrection event was admirable and life-changing for all those who saw it then, and believed. It's admirable and life-changing for us who live 2,000 years after the events of that day, and who choose to believe now by faith. "Admirable" was a descriptive word then; it's a descriptive word now.

"Deserving of the highest esteem" is an accurate way to illustrate "Admirable," according to the dictionary. This trait is for us to contemplate and upon which to act.

I imagine you or others you know have attended an amusement fair where a roller coaster is part of the entertainment package for attendees. One of the most well-known rollercoasters in the world, still operational in this day and age, is located in Belmont Park in San Diego, California. The ride, aptly named the Giant Big Dipper, is set apart because of its age. It was constructed in 1925, and officially opened on July 4th of that year. The ride is a part of the Mission Beach Amusement Center.

I have enjoyed this ride several times. *It is admirable because it is surprising*! Fortunately, construction is solid, and remains so to this day.

What we witness here: the trait of admirable can be used to describe all kinds of unusual characteristics, events, and experiences that inspire wonder, if not awe. One more thing: this rollercoaster ride certainly is of "highest esteem;" one reason: it takes patrons *very high,* and fortunately brings them down safely.

Yes, the term "admirable" is descriptive of several things. Among them:

1. God's character, our example to emulate
2. The side-by-side comparison of God's eternal existence to a time of human loss
3. Life-change brought about in a remarkable salvation event
4. God's provision when the source of that provision is unknown
5. The Resurrection of Christ
6. Our acceptance by faith of the validity of Christ's returning to life
7. The surprise of a rollercoaster ride

To what degree do we long to witness and participate in the multiple aspects of admirability, which is one of eight listed for us in Philippians 4:8?

Admirable

I pray this is more than a passing and fanciful list of descriptive terms. May the list of traits created by the Apostle Paul, become ingrained in us to the glory of God and may permanent life change result!

*****

Chapter Seven
Excellent

It's Time to Stand UP

By Mickey Straub
President, Sales Activity Management, Inc.
Mayor Emeritus/Author/Patriot
Congressional Record Recipient

When my dear friend, kindred spirit, and Brother in Christ, Glen Aubrey, asked me to join his inner circle of accomplished authors and friends, to write this chapter about thinking and being "Excellent," I had a myriad of excuses not to do it. They ranged from "I have too many other priorities and don't have enough time" to "I am not good enough or worthy."

As I resisted—and Glen persisted—I had this gnawing feeling that God wanted me to do this. Then another realization hit me that, though my business might be all about pursuing excellence and doing your best, there are times that I have not been following my own advice.

Well, you can see how that worked out for me.

All of us must think differently than we often do in our pursuit of excellence and resist that negative self-talk that we all hear sometimes. My resistance to write this chapter was one such shining moment, but Paul's words that Glen captured from Philippians Chapter 4:8 in the first few pages, kept echoing in my ears:

> **Finally, brothers and sisters ...** *Whatever is true, Whatever is noble, Whatever is right, Whatever is pure, Whatever is lovely, Whatever is admirable, If anything is* <u>EXCELLENT</u> *Or praiseworthy, Think about such things."*

Why did the Apostle Paul give us that advice or directive? Why did he tell us to think about whatever is true, noble, right, pure, admirable, excellent, and praiseworthy?

The first thing that came to my mind was a motivational recording that I heard as an early teenager, a timeless message that I have listened to countless times and that has made a huge impact in my life. It is called ***The Strangest Secret*** by Earl Nightingale, and it was the first Gold Record self-improvement audio tape of its kind.

What is the Strangest Secret with which he inspired now millions of people? Simply put, it is this:

<u>**"We become what we think about."**</u>

Excellent

According to Mr. Nightingale, it is "strange" because it is a well-known truism agreed upon by virtually all philosophers and wise men, yet it virtually remains a "secret" to most people.

I saw how true this principle was in my very own family seventeen years ago. My niece was a troubled teenager after her parents got divorced and she started hanging out with the wrong crowd. She dropped out of college, lost her license after getting two DUI's (Driving Under the Influence), did not have a job, was living in the basement of her mother's townhome, and got pregnant out of wedlock.

I offered to help her by paying her to read books and extra money for doing a review and to help her get financially on her feet.

The first book she chose to read and summarize (much to my surprise) was **As A Man Thinketh**, by James Allen ... and it changed her life. In her first summary, she wrote, "Changing my thought process has also given me a purpose in my life and the power to try to achieve it. Even if I fail, I will keep trying and won't give up until I have accomplished everything that I set out to achieve. This will help build my strength and my character to the person I want to be. **As A Man Thinketh**, although not a very large book, has completely changed my thoughts and my character."

To make a long story short, she proactively walked into a real estate office (instead of applying online) and got a job as a receptionist. She eventually became a real estate agent and a very successful sales representative in another industry earning more than she ever originally thought possible. On top of that, she raised two wonderful children on her own (in Catholic school), went back to church, reunited with a high school friend, fell in love, and they are happily married. This is the power of thinking differently.

One can only assume that Apostle Paul knew this when he told his followers to **"Think about these things,"** and the impact doing so could have on one's life and society in general. Chances are he was exposed to the concept of "becoming what you think about" since it was even addressed in the book of Proverbs about 700 years earlier:

Proverbs 23:7 (NKJV)

For as he thinks in his heart, so *is* he.

~ Scripture taken from the New King James Version®. Copyright © 1982 by Thomas Nelson. Used by permission. All rights reserved.

(As a footnote, my guess is that Earl Nightingale's inspiring words were rooted in scripture, as are most of the motivational, self-improvement messages we hear today.)

The Apostle Paul knew that we move in the direction of our most dominant thoughts so that by "thinking about such

Excellent

things" such as being "Excellent," we would eventually become it. He told us what to think for our own good, but I suspect the other reason he chose those words is because he wanted to assist (and encourage) us in our pursuit of heaven.

Yes, Paul told us *what* to think but, in many ways, he was also telling us *how* to think. What a gift! He also knew something that I just learned recently in a book called **Fast-Starting a Career of Consequence** by Fred Sievert. In it he quoted Arthur Miller's interpretation of Matthew 16:27: *"We will be held accountable for our giftedness."* What a concept and motivator for us all to "think about these things" and to use all of our God-given gifts to the best of our ability… because we are going to be held accountable.

Miller's words also reminded me of a quote by Rick Warren that I heard many years ago that — if and when we get to heaven — God will ask us two crucial things:

1. What did you do with My Son, Jesus Christ?
2. What did you do with My gifts?

When Glen asked me to write this chapter, he said, "I have chosen you to invite you to do this because you are excellent." While that was a nice thought and a welcome compliment, excellence is never revealed in arrogance, self-aggrandizement, or bragging. I am no different than anyone else, certainly not "better" in any way. But in the end, I decided to follow where I thought that God was leading me (which I have been trying to do for years) and share some things that I think (and hope) God wants more people to hear.

Guilt was also a motivator "to be better at practicing what I preach." (But then again, as a Catholic Christian, "I am trained to feel guilty" as the joke goes. It worked.)

So, what does it mean to be "Excellent" and was the Apostle Paul referring to only our thoughts or our actions, too?

As Glen indicated, "Excellent" is an *adjective* meaning "being of great virtue or worth; eminent or distinguished for what is amiable, valuable or laudable." ~ Merriam-Webster 1828

In addition, I found the following definitions: "possessing outstanding quality or superior merit; remarkably good and extraordinary."

The opposites (or antonyms) of "Excellent" are equally descriptive, if not diametrically opposed: atrocious, awful, and lousy. But even less dramatic terms like "mediocre" should inspire most people of reason to want to aspire to be excellent in all aspects of their lives.

After all, who wants to be considered mediocre? Not me. That is certainly one of the last words that I would like to have included in my eulogy, and I trust the same goes for you.

Excellent

Literally, Paul only referred to what we should "think." But his push for us toward excellence would have to include both, since "thinking is always a precursor to activity" and, as we have seen, can dramatically impact our activity and results.

James helps us connect the dots, also, when he tells us that, while we are saved by faith, not deeds, he states assuredly that faith without works doesn't work.

James 2:17 (NIV):

> In the same way faith by itself, if it is not accompanied by action, is dead.

At a minimum, mediocrity is the enemy of excellence and, in our working for the Lord, mediocrity is never an option. When we consider excellence, by definition, we are not contemplating anything less in what we 'think and do' in all aspects of life. A pursuit of excellence is God's command. Our responsibility is to obey. This is an eternal principle from God, Himself.

Once again, in our working for the Lord, mediocrity is never an option. God's will and desire for us is to be Christ-like and to have eternal life with Him in heaven. That must be our goal and is, after all, why Jesus died for us on the cross.

Was Paul referring to our work, personal or spiritual lives, or all of the above?

Here is some good news: Excellence does not mean perfection. God does not expect us to be perfect, which the Apostle Paul and the other saints knew from personal experience. But God does expect us to pursue perfection and to be "excellent" in our efforts to be Christ-like in all aspects of our life as we pursue eternal life in heaven with Him.

Out of all Paul's directives, this one resonates with me most and reminds me of Lexus' marketing slogan: "The Relentless Pursuit of Perfection." It also inspires us to try our best to achieve the most and regret the least in this earthly life, and to do the best with God's gifts in our pursuit of heaven ... and to please Jesus if, and when, we arrive.

The pursuit of excellence in this chapter also has a lot to do with what I do for a living. In 1995, I founded a company based on helping sales professionals become their best using a concept and strategy we named "Activity Management," because activities produce results. The better you manage activities, the better the results.

And it is probably no coincidence it has biblical roots. After all, Jesus made it clear in Galatians 6:7 that "Whatsoever a man soweth, that shall he also reap." (KJV)

In shorter terms, **we reap what we sow**.

It all starts with how you think, and it applies to virtually all aspects of life, from counting steps and calories, to praying

Excellent

the Rosary, and to every sport and profession. If you, or anyone you know, is interested in learning more about this empowering concept and pragmatic approach to pursuing excellence in any endeavor, I can be reached at Mickey.Straub@SAMusa.com or by calling (630) 645-1726.

We are a patriotic, faith-based company; the website address is www.SalesActivityManagement and the shortcut is www.SAMusa.com.

There is such a profound need and a cry for excellence in our world, especially these days! At the time of this writing, America is still recovering from the deadly effects of the Covid 19 pandemic and shutdowns, and I'm not just applying this to the mortality rates.

One of the grave side effects of all this is that we know both a quality and quantity crisis when it comes to excellence, or the lack thereof. Far too many workers are not performing their jobs excellently (mediocre at best), and many people are unwilling to work at all.

The latter got even worse. The government increased and extended the unemployment benefits and gave so many "handouts" that many people made more money if they stayed home instead of going to work. As always, a satisfied need is no longer motivating.

This lack of excellence is evident both in the workplace and our places of worship, and I'm not sure which one was harder hit. With the majority of churches being either shuttered temporarily or permanently, it was as if it was all intended to put a wedge between man and God, and it worked. We know this was part of God's sovereign plan, and hope it will reverse soon, and the world will be better off, but it has been painful to watch.

Thankfully, it has had the opposite effect in some places, where it has ignited people's faith and church attendance. I know of one church that doubled in size since the shutdowns started, and I hope there are many more of which I am unaware. And, hopefully, the silent majority is still the majority ... and they are finally waking up.

*****

> **What did you do with My Son, Jesus Christ, and what did you do with My gifts?**

Those are two great questions and worth repeating because they both lead back to our pursuit of excellence, to "think about such things" and, ultimately, to become them. They also remind us of "Why" we should do it, which fuels our fire to take action.

Though, in the end, the "What" is probably as equally important as the "How." So how do we become "Excellent"

Excellent

in our personal, professional, and spiritual endeavors? What are the best steps, tips, and keys? And is there a magic formula?

Far be it for me to claim that I have all the answers to these vital questions. I do not. As a matter of fact, I would bet that there have been hundreds, if not thousands of books written on this subject by people far more educated, wise, accomplished, wealthier, and successful than I have been blessed to become.

But I would like to address the one thing upon which excellence is built that might get overlooked. It is the one principle or value upon which excellence is also measured. It is the one thing that I didn't even know was of so much importance to me until I read a book many years ago called *The Path*, by Laurie Beth Jones.

The subtitle of her book is "Creating Your Mission Statement for Work and Life" which gives you a good idea of its content and purpose. Though I do not recall the exact details about the exercise in her book, the question that was asked was something like, "What principle or value is so important to you that you would go to your deathbed to prevent it from being eliminated from society?"

After reviewing the list of alternatives, the answer that I came up with was this: **TRUTH**.

So, what does truth have to do with excellence? In a word, *everything!* The only way one's performance in any endeavor can be determined is if it is being based on accuracy, i.e., truth. Of course, things like desire, commitment, action, measurement are all needed, but <u>the foundation of it all has to be truth</u>.

Truth is the first prerequisite. Without accuracy, there can be no truth. Without truth, there can be no excellence. Without measurement, there can be no accuracy. Without desire, there will be no effort (action).

One of my dear friends, Padraic O'Connor (a carpenter from Ireland) put it best in a recent conversation when he said, "You can't be excellent without embracing the truth. They are not separate issues; you can't have one without the other. Truth is a destination. Excellence is the journey; it's where you make changes and become better people: by embracing the truth."

He also added: "Confusion (of truth) is one of the tools that Satan uses to destroy society."

I couldn't agree with him more in all aspects of life! We have to have a standard on which we compare ourselves, and it has to be based on TRUTH.

The Decline of Excellence and Truth

Excellent

Whatever is True is a fitting title for this book since truth applies to all of its precepts, especially when it comes to being "Excellent." With "excellence and truth" being such important principles in my life, you can imagine how difficult it has been for me to watch what has been happening in America over the last couple of years. In your lifetime, did you ever think that you'd see such a decline of excellence in our society?

For example:

Did you think that your government would:

1. Confine you to your home?
2. Prevent you from being able to see sickly loved ones in hospitals or nursing homes?
3. Stop you from attending church or receiving communion?

Did you ever think:

1. We would see our national monuments being destroyed or protesters be allowed to freely loot businesses, injure at will, or attack police officers without punishment?
2. Politicians could get away with telling lies about their opponents with no proof or consequence?
3. Spiritual tepidity (lukewarmness) would be so widespread in America that belief in God and heaven

would wane, and people would stop practicing their faith?

Would you ever expect that in America, a federal agency that oversaw disease control could:

1. Decide if your job was essential or non-essential?
2. Force you to wear a face mask that was as effective at preventing a virus from spreading as a chain link fence would be to keep out mosquitos?
3. Mandate you to get a vaccine that did not vaccinate?
4. Then make it financially attractive for all medical facilities to attribute virtually all of the deaths to the new virus (COVID 19) and none to the old one (Influenza) even though the symptoms were the same, and even many with none as long as they tested positive?

I recall Glen praying: "Father, thank You for Mickey. Thank You for his life and testimony." I responded, "I have an overwhelming and great desire to serve God and to be obedient." This commitment is what we consider to be a model of excellence.

There are times when you and I may feel unworthy of God's call to excellence. We may possess doubts of our abilities to do "excellence" for God. Even Moses felt he didn't have the capacity to speak well, but God used him excellently to accomplish His will as long as Moses obeyed.

Excellent

We have responsibilities God calls us to accomplish for Him. Often, we are "pastor/shepherds" to those we touch, especially to those we lead. People look at us as pacemakers who are doing God's work. (Glen observed regarding me: "That is why you became mayor of your town, traveled to 50 Capitols in 50 days, and it's why you are a big fan of Abraham Lincoln, who 'pastored' America with inspiration and guidance in the country's most crucial era, the Civil War.")

In the truest definition, a pastor is a shepherd who leads by example. Shepherds communicate to their sheep, their flocks, using their voice alone. Of course, the sheep have to listen!

We are like sheep, and as sheep, we are to listen and receive the shepherd's truth. Then, we must "think about these things" that we've heard. This becomes our prelude to the actions following the model of the shepherd.

Will all of us sometimes fail or not perform as "excellently" as we would like to? Sure. But we can all pick ourselves up and keep trying in our pursuit of perfection: heaven.

As Christ followers, our call is to deal honestly with each other, in obedience to God. This lifestyle is all about "whatever is true."

Determining "excellence" can be subjective and based on opinions and preferences unless strict, uniform measurement procedures are in place with no variations. But "Truth" is an absolute; either something is true or it's not.

*****

So, what is truth, real truth? This book is called "Holistic" for an important reason. Truth is listed in Philippians 4:8 *first* in a lineup of important and vital characteristics of living according to the pattern established by Christ.

Who does this concern? Well, the "audience" for this book is everyone who cares enough to dare to speak, act, believe, and showcase truth in personal life and in front of God and others.

Jesus set the standard for us when it came to truth. In John 8:31 and 32 Jesus said to the Jews who had believed him, "If you abide in my word, you are truly my disciples, [32] and you will know the truth, and the truth will set you free." And in John 18:37, Jesus told Pilate: "The reason I was born and came into the world is to testify to the truth. Everyone on the side of truth listens to me."

Unfortunately, the decline in truthfulness in America has been increasing at what feels like Mach 1 Speed in recent years. These days, if a man puts on a dress, the liberals want

Excellent

you to believe that he's a woman. That's a lie and pure craziness, and all of this is an assault on God.

They are turning truth upside down to distract people. I saw this firsthand while the mayor of a prominent Chicago suburb and during my visits to the state capitol; when the politicians on the left (mostly) would repeat a lie often enough some people would accept it as the truth no matter how blatant.

Did you ever think that well-intentioned, liberal citizens would:

1. Believe and push that there are more than two (2) genders in the human race, let alone seventy-two (72), which they now claim? God created two (2) genders: male and female. (Genesis 1:27)
2. Encourage and openly promote homosexuality and gay marriage on television, in parades, and in the movies in the name of equality to the detriment of the family?

Truth is now subjective, at least that's what liberals want you to think. Here is their modus operandi—Deny, Distort, and Distract—and the name of the one responsible begins with the same letter, the "Devil." I guess that shouldn't surprise us since, as Jesus told the Jews in John 8:44 (NIV):

"When he (Satan) lies, he speaks his native language, for he is a liar and the father of lies."

Did you ever think you would see the day when the integrity of our (coveted) democratic elections would be called into question?

Did you ever think that public schools would ever allow boys to compete in girls' sports, or put sanitary napkins in the boys' bathrooms, or allow boys to have access to girls' bathrooms? The latter was confirmed by a friend in Chicago who asked her sixteen-year-old female employee why she was dressing so promiscuously? She told her that the same boys who play for the football team on the weekend come into school on Monday and claim "Gender Dysphoria," i.e., they "feel" like a girl that day, so they can access the girls' room to have sex with a willing partner.

She wants to be one of them. I'm not making this stuff up ... it's happening!

Thank God that Roe vs. Wade was recently overturned by the U. S. Supreme Court, which shows some promise that truth and excellence may be coming back in vogue!

Abortion is such a violation of both, and I hope that in the year 2122, people will look back and say, "Do you mean that Americans 100 years ago actually murdered millions of innocent, defenseless babies under the guise of calling it a mother's "Choice", and claiming that a baby in a mother's womb was not considered to be a human being?" What about the baby's choice? God's choice?

I heard Dennis Prager say that what he likes to ask liberals is this: "If it's not a human being, then what is it? Is it a zygote? A pimple?" Crickets. That's all he could hear. I have often wondered, "Why do liberals only point to "Science" when it fits their narrative and agenda? Well, I guess we all know the answer to that one.

"Claiming there are more than two genders" is another ridiculous and indefensible position when it comes to science or common sense. Bluntly put, **it's an outright lie** and the same goes for anyone claiming they can change their gender because of how they "feel," whether it's for a day, month, year, or a lifetime. Just because I wake up "feeling like an Astronaut" doesn't mean that I can fly to the moon!

Excellence and truth are synonymous, and there is a profound need for more of both in today's world! Did you ever think that you would hear so many half-truths, non-truths, twisted truths, and outright lies so pervasively in our society being spread by even government officials, federal agencies, and media outlets? Where is the higher standard today?

This is the devil's handiwork, and we would all do well to remind ourselves of how Reverend Anthony J. Paone, S. J. put it in his book called **My Daily Bread**. He described the devil as "The enemy of Truth" and Jesus as "The Author of Truth."

<u>Unfortunately, liberals have taken lying to a new art form, much like the Communists did in the 1940s.</u>

*****

As I write this chapter and think of what we have seen change over the last couple of years with societal norms and the socialist policies being implemented — along with the plummeting stock market (down 33%), the near doubling of food prices, and tripling of gasoline prices plus the highest inflation rate in 50 years — an old movie called *Network* comes to mind. It is the scene, and memorable plea, of a News Reporter, Howard Beale (played by Peter Finch), while he's delivering his *Evening News*:

Speech from *Network* (1976 film)

"I don't have to tell you that things are bad. Everybody knows things are bad. It's a depression. Everybody's out of work or scared of losing their job. The dollar buys a nickel's worth. Banks are going bust. Shopkeepers are keeping guns under the counter. Punks are running wild in the street and there's nobody anywhere seems to know what to do and there's no end to it.

Excellent

"We sit watching our TV's while some local newscaster tells us that today we had 15 homicides and 63 violent crimes as if that's the way it's supposed to be. We know things are bad, worse than bad, they're crazy! It's like everything everywhere is going crazy so we don't go out anymore. We sit in the house and slowly the world we're living in gets smaller, and all we say is, 'Please, at least let us leave our living rooms. I won't say anything. Just leave us alone.' Well, I'm not going to leave you alone! I want you to get mad!

"I don't want you to protest, I don't want you to riot. I don't know what to do about the depression and the inflation and the Russians and the crime in the street. All I know is first you've got to get mad! So, I want you to get up now! I want all of you to get up out of your chairs, I want you to get up right now and go to the window, open it, and stick your head out and yell: 'I'm as mad as hell, and I'm not going to take this anymore!'

© Speech from Network (1976) https://www.youtube.com/watch?v=ZwMVMbmQBug

If we were to do a remake of that movie today, the storyline wouldn't change much, only now some things seem even worse! You would think that we would have learned, but history has a way of repeating itself.

Our public education system is an abject failure and control of illegal immigration has been destroyed. We face crises in mental health, suicide, drug addiction, and homelessness, and that's just for starters.

The flood of district attorneys who refuse to prosecute crimes has led to a huge rise in violent crime. Chicago alone, which is just fifteen miles away from my home, has seen the number of homicides skyrocket. The city has recorded nearly 770 homicides in 2020, up 50% from the previous year! The *Chicago Tribune* even reported last year the city broke a 25-year record when it surpassed 800 homicides. That's over two per day! Those in charge try to blame it on systemic racism, but that's a lie since 97% of homicides and shooters were black, as are virtually all of the Windy City's top government and political leaders.

The recent pandemic also revealed a stunningly incompetent health system that probably killed more people in nursing homes than it saved, while counting anyone who died as victims of COVID because they tested positive, even though they actually drowned or died in a motorcycle accident. And with all the fearmongering that the government has peddled, two years later many people are still too scared

Excellent

to go to social gatherings, to work, or drive a car alone, without wearing a mask (which drives me crazy), or even leave their home.

If that all is not enough — when it comes to the lack of truth and excellence — to get every American mad, I don't know what is! But there is one possible explanation, and it is explained in this old story:

> A guy was walking down the street and, when he was about to pass by an old man's house, he noticed there was a dog on his porch that was barking and howling, barking and howling. So, he asked, "Excuse me old man, but why is your dog barking and howling?" The man replied, "Well, it's because he's sitting on a nail." Perplexed, the guy asked, "But, why doesn't he get off the nail?" The old man said, "Because it doesn't hurt bad enough yet."

That must be it ... as bad as it is, **"It doesn't hurt bad enough yet."**

Maybe the decline of truth and excellence — along with morals and freedoms — has happened so slowly that it doesn't hurt bad enough? Hopefully, now that more parents have learned how our educators are teaching our second-grade children about transgenderism, gender dysphoria, using sexually explicit photographs that would be considered pornographic if presented by a stranger at the library, plus the alleged "systemic racism" and anti-American propaganda that our public (and some private) schools are peddling, <u>maybe will that finally be enough to get people mad</u>?

Oh, how I wish that every American could have heard just a fraction of the warnings that I have heard from immigrants about how they are seeing things the very same things in America that caused them to leave their own countries. Here's one of the most glaring examples that got my attention and it happened at the barber shop last summer:

> As I was sitting in the barber chair, unmasked per usual, I noticed a fully masked Asian man come in, sit down, and stare at me — at least that is what it felt like he was doing! Feeling a bit uncomfortable, and wanting to be sensitive to his concerns, I was almost out the door when I heard him say something to the other barber about how crazy this pandemic was. So, I stopped and confirmed what I heard. Then he said something that I will never, ever forget...
>
>> "I moved here from China 30 years ago, and I have to tell you that America is looking more and more like China these days and, unless you white guys start standing up, we're screwed!"

Excellent

(That was not what I expected...especially coming from a Chinese guy!)

It's time to get mad, and it's time to stand up!

It's time to think differently than society is directing us to think.

It's time for America to turn back to God, instead of turning their backs on God.

It's time to "Think about whatever is true ... and excellent" as the Apostle Paul directed us.

It's time for all people to stand up, and not just the white guys!

It's time for every white, black, brown, and yellow person -- no matter what race, color or creed -- to stand up as one!
E Pluribus Unum.

It's time for all teachers and all government and private industry employees to stand up!

It's time for each American, every factory worker, farmer, soldier, policeman, fireman, salesperson, pilot, athlete, doctor, nurse, barista, and bagger to stand up for truth and excellence, as if eternal life, the future, and the sovereignty of our nation depend on it!

Mickey Straub

They do depend on it … and it's time to stand up.

*****

My Bout with COVID

I wasn't planning on relating my COVID story (including an 11-day hospital stay), but it seems only fitting.

In early August of 2021, I started feeling sick with what I thought were flu symptoms. As usual, I tried to fight them off by improving my diet and sleep habits, but my condition continued to worsen. Finally, after several days of my wife telling me to get tested, I went into a Loyola facility and, sure enough, I tested positive for COVID.

Always the optimist, and reluctant to seek medical attention, I continued with over-the-counter medications and my own treatments, plus added a plethora of natural remedies, courtesy of a dear friend (Thank you, Sam!), all unsuccessfully. After a few more days of a fever and worsening symptoms, my wife and I sat down for lunch at the kitchen table. It was then I realized that I just didn't have enough energy to even eat.

So, after over a week of trying to fight COVID off, I finally gave in to having her drive me to the Palos Community Hospital, which was just being bought out and taken over by Northwestern Medicine.

Excellent

When I arrived at the Emergency Room, I was even weaker, and again didn't have the energy to eat, or even fight. My energy level was so depleted that I didn't know if I would ever recover.

I had reached a point of accepting whatever outcome God had in store for me, just as Jesus had taught us to do in the Lord's Prayer from His Sermon on the Mount: "Thy will be done." It was a scary, but peaceful feeling.

Thankfully, there were many of the old guard there, my wife's fellow co-workers, still working at the main hospital (that was originally Catholic) for which my wife, Charmaine, had worked as a Registered Nurse for over forty years. That was comforting and made my transition from freedom to isolation I was about to endure, a lot easier. Though I never thought (should I recover) that I would not be allowed to see family or friends for longer than a few days, let alone for over a week!

Chest X-Rays showed that I had bilateral pneumonia and, as my wife had already confirmed, "my lungs, sounded like crackling glass." In addition, I was running a high fever and suffered from dehydration.

My team of doctors immediately put me on IV fluids and 24/7 oxygen beginning at 2-3 liters. They then quickly raised it up to 11 liters for most of my stay. (I was told that this was the highest level allowed nasally, right below requiring a metal mask, then a ventilator.) I also took vitamins C, D, E, and Zinc daily, and they put me on a steroid called Decadron, plus infusions of Remdesivir, a drug with anti-viral benefits.

From day one, I asked about Hydroxychloroquine and Ivermectin, which was how President Donald Trump had been treated for COVID. But three out of my four doctors kept telling me that they would not recommend it, that their medical society advised against it, and that it was not an option.

In addition, I did not know, and was not told, that Remdesivir was quite controversial and known to have serious, and even lethal, side effects, like kidney failure. One could argue that the use of both drugs was subjective, but truth and excellence were also called into question.

Having made little progress, on day five I agreed with my primary pulmonologist, Dr. Samran Haider, for me to start taking an experimental drug, Barcitinib, that was not approved by the FDA for COVID, though it was commonly used for rheumatoid arthritis and approved through an EUA (Emergency Use Authorization). I was told that Barcitinib was used for decreasing inflammation in the lungs and body, but had the side effect of lowering the immune system. There was another drug, Actemra, that they wanted to use first, but there was a national shortage and it was unavailable.

Excellent

On the day I started on Barcitinib my health started to improve. This was also the day that I started to <u>think differently</u>.

Up until day five, and for the first time in my life, I hadn't shaved, brushed my hair, or even really bathed. (The hospital staff did a great job, but my hygiene or bed sheets were not priorities for them.) After I changed my attitude, shaved, washed my hair and body, started to do light exercise daily, plus do breathing exercises (three sets, eight times a day) and remained prone (laying on my stomach) for 12-16 hours a day, I started feeling better consistently, day by day. (I was kept on 11 liters of oxygen, but my pulse oxygen level gradually improved a little every day.)

Constantly, I told every doctor, nurse, nurse's aide, and even the staff delivering the food, about how long my wife had worked there, how excited I was about my faith, and how much I appreciated what they were doing for me. Besides all that being true, it pays dividends to have friends and to be nice!

The other thing that I did was "Focus on Jesus" from Day One, and I prayed the Rosary every day! I had only brought two pieces of reading material with me when I scrambled to leave my home: a Knights of Columbus ***Columbia Magazine*** and a little book called, ***What does Jesus mean to me?*** (I had received the latter back in 2008 from a born-again Christian friend of mine, the late Charlie "Tremendous" Jones, and had finally completed reading it during my stay.)

I also binged on Christian movies every night by watching every episode of Seasons One and Two of **The Chosen** (for the second time) and streamed **Pureflix** movies with my iPhone. I'll never forget the one line in one of their movies from a former Hell's Angel motorcycle guy turned Christian, who would ask perfect strangers, "Hey, do you know Jesus?"

The last thing I ever expected to do while in the hospital was to focus on Jesus for ten straight days, or to evangelize from my hospital bed, but that's exactly what I did.

Was it a miracle for me to leave the hospital after eleven days of receiving the maximum level of oxygen which can be administered nasally, with no restrictions and requiring only one prescription for baby aspirin?

I don't know. But what I do know is this: <u>thinking (and doing) differently were the turning points</u>. I also believe that praying every day, focusing on Jesus, and having prayer groups of friends and family all over the country pray for my survival, was the difference maker. I also suspect that praying the Rosary every day for the previous nine years, which included deep breathing exercises and meditation, helped prepare and strengthen my lungs for what I was to go through.

Excellent

"When air becomes the priority, everything changes, and my priorities have changed forever." COVID was a blessing, and a curse. There were times that I was tempted to give up, but God had other plans. There was also one more thing that happened that was so timely it was uncanny, serendipitous, and we think providential, that has to do with the picture on the next page.

Charmaine's Sign

Three days after I was admitted to the hospital, Charmaine, my wife, had been home recovering from her milder case of Covid. She was distraught and worried about whether or not I would survive.

She decided to get out of the house, reasoning it would be safe for her to take a drive by herself in her convertible, to get some fresh air.

Charmaine drove south on Route 83 and took a right at the Clark Gas Station toward the Waterfall Glen Forest Preserve. As she made the curve north toward the Argonne National Laboratory property, she noticed the beautiful, bright blue sky ahead of her which reminded her of a picture I had taken of her during a visit to Sedona, Arizona a few years earlier. She decided to drive in its direction.

Charmaine Straub, Sedona Arizona

Along the way, she thought to herself, "If Mickey gets through this, we'll have to go back there to visit."

Instead of heading toward home, she drove toward where the sky was bluest, making a left at the first light and pulled into the National Shrine of Saint Therese. Though it was located at Our Lady of Mt. Carmel in Darien, Illinois, not far away, she never knew then that shrine even existed.

She sat in the gazebo, prayed for my recovery, and cried. Then she stood in front of the statue of St. Teresa of Avila that she felt drawn to, prayed again, and took a walk around the grounds to see the many other statues. Along the way, she stopped and prayed to God that He would restore my health because my work here was not yet completed.

Excellent

Charmaine then drove home, pulled into the garage, and went about her day. A few hours later, her phone randomly dinged and, for no particular reason, up came the very same picture that I took of her in Sedona that she was thinking about when she was driving to the Shrine!!

That was Charmaine's Sign. To her it said, "Mickey was going to be okay."

Her entire outlook changed, and so did my health; it was the day before my turnaround began.

Charmaine and Mickey Straub, Sedona, Arizona

It is worth noting, during my last, post-hospital visit with one of my doctors, that he was adamant about me getting the COVID vaccine, and he continued to minimize the role of natural immunity.

So, I asked him, "Doc, does the vaccine guarantee that someone who takes this vaccine won't get COVID?" He said, "No." Next, I asked, "Does it guarantee that one taking the vaccine can't carry COVID?" Once again, he said, "No." Then, I asked, "Does the vaccine guarantee that I can't transmit COVID if I take it?" He said, "No."

So, then I asked him, "If the vaccine doesn't vaccinate, why would I ever want to get the vaccine?" The best answer he could give was this: "To minimize future symptoms and to avoid the side effects of the drugs they will give you to get over COVID."

After finding out that he had a young daughter, I asked him, "Are you going to get her vaccinated?" He said, "No." As I am sure you have already guessed, I chose the same answer for me, and discouraged vaccine use at my household.

Unfortunately, what is convincing is too often believed over the truth. That was one of my final lessons in public office, and was certainly the case when it came to the pandemic.

It's time for everyone to
<u>Stand Up for Truth and Excellence.</u>

How Glen and I met:

The short answer would probably be "through Divine Intervention." It sure felt that way, when by complete chance, we met at the Gettysburg Hotel in 2013. I still remember the table he was sitting at in the restaurant, which can't be said of all my first encounters.

Glen and I are kindred spirits in many ways. To begin with, we are both huge fans of Abraham Lincoln who, not surprisingly, introduced us, at least indirectly. We both went to Gettysburg for the 150th anniversary of the Gettysburg Address and all the festivities surrounding it.

We spoke for quite a while about Abraham Lincoln, and I was absolutely stunned to meet someone with such a deep knowledge and understanding of him, especially when I'd already heard of the many books and articles Glen had written about our 16th President.

It was then that our connection became even deeper when we compared notes on Christianity and how we both chose to follow God's lead. I was also incredibly touched by a dear friend of his with whom we had dinner. I so wish I had recorded Nancy Sidock's prayers for me that night, which seemed to continue fueling my faith and self-confidence, confirming I was on the right path.

I am so blessed to have kept in contact with Glen over the years and so appreciate his advice on the printing of my first book, as well as his enthusiasm for love of God and country which we both share.

He is truly one of America's unsung heroes.

~ Mickey Straub, July, 2022

<u>Glen's recollection of meeting Mickey Straub and a continuing association:</u>

I well recall the first occasions of interaction with Mickey Straub in Gettysburg, Pennsylvania. I was staying at the Gettysburg Hotel to be available to display and offer for sale the books on Lincoln I had been privileged to write and publish.

Several books were offered: *Lincoln, Leadership and Gettysburg * Defining Moments of Greatness; Lessons of War * Lincoln's Second Inaugural Address, Leadership at Gettysburg; Lincoln * The Making of a Leader; Lincoln's Leadership * If You Want Success, Lead Like This;* and *Lincoln's Advice for America in the 21st Century * His Words Still Speak.*

From the outset, I was impressed with Mickey's unyielding dedication to truth, American History (including Lincoln), his patriotism, love for our freedoms and the prices paid to secure those freedoms, and his profound belief in God, submission to Him, and his love for the redemptive work of Jesus Christ.

Because America was built on the values of God as proclaimed by our Founding Fathers, both Mickey and I seek to tell the truth, expose voluminous liberal lies, and help to bring America "back home" to the Godly foundations of her birth.

America, its military, its citizenry, and its values are being assaulted today, as many have expressed in this book already. **We must stand up for Truth**. **We must rise up for Excellence**.

Philippians 4:8 brought these truths and others together through the writings of the Apostle Paul, penned more than 2,000 years ago. Although he didn't have America in mind when he wrote this passage, in truth it is applicable today to the issues our Godly nation faces. This scripture has become a spiritual and living template of Divine truths for us to read, consider, follow, and share with others.

Finally, a word about Nancy Sidock who today remains a close mentor of mine. She is a spiritual poet and "prophetess," an outstanding personal contributor of faith, and a powerful prayer partner. I am honored and blessed whenever she and I have opportunities to converse on the phone.

The combination of Nancy, Mickey, and Glen is a blessing almost beyond words.

~ Glen Aubrey, July, 2022

Chapter Eight
Praiseworthy
Meditate on Praiseworthy

By Jim Robeson
President and CEO
Robeson and Associates, Inc.

Early in my married life we confronted a major family crisis. My whole life was rocked to the core, and I wasn't sure what to expect going forward.

I had come to Christ several years earlier, but I was still trying to find my way in my walk with Jesus. What I didn't know then, but I know now is that *all* of Christ's followers experience trials and tribulations.

See James 1:2-7 (NIV):

> [2] Consider it pure joy, my brothers and sisters, whenever you face trials of many kinds, [3] because you know that the testing of your faith produces perseverance.

> ⁴ Let perseverance finish its work so that you may be mature and complete, not lacking anything. ⁵ If any of you lacks wisdom, you should ask God, who gives generously to all without finding fault, and it will be given to you. ⁶ But when you ask, you must believe and not doubt, because the one who doubts is like a wave of the sea, blown and tossed by the wind. ⁷ That person should not expect to receive anything from the Lord.

Fortunately, my father-in-law and spiritual father, Dr. Robert Luther, was there to help me through this family crisis. I was reading my Bible and attending a Bible study, but I hadn't learned the habit of memorizing or meditating on Scripture.

One day, while speaking with Dr. Luther, he gave me a great piece of advice ... "Memorize and meditate on Philippians 4:8." He encouraged me to add the habits of memorizing and meditating on this verse *daily*.

He explained that my mind was becoming a reservoir of Biblical truth as I heard, read, studied, and absorbed God's Word. But those truths needed to be thought through, pondered, personalized, and applied to every part of my life.

They would replace the alien and demoralizing thoughts of this family crisis that were traveling through my mind all day, every day. Dr. Luther is now with Jesus in heaven. I can't thank Dr. Luther enough for his wisdom to think on "that which is excellent and praiseworthy" ... God's Word and His words.

My Dream — Praiseworthy

<u>The Current Family Crisis</u>

What does "praiseworthy" mean? And for that matter what isn't "praiseworthy?"

First, by definition, "praiseworthy" is something that is admirable, creditable, awesome, worthy, or deserving. The opposite is defined as something that is contemptible, despicable, vile, or dishonorable.

When Dr. Luther suggested that I memorize and meditate on what is "excellent or praiseworthy" I had to really understand both ... <u>what it was and what it wasn't</u>. Because the family crisis was ever-present in my mind, I chose to start with what was so "un-praiseworthy" about this issue ... I questioned, "Why was this so insidious?"

Probably for the first time in my Christian walk I was truly experiencing what the Bible calls spiritual warfare. What is spiritual warfare? Did I really believe that there was such a thing?

As I read and studied the Bible, I saw that the Apostle Paul spoke specifically about this in Ephesians 6:10-20 and defined it in verse 12 (NIV):

> 12 For our struggle is not against flesh and blood, but against the rulers, against the authorities, against the powers of this dark world and against the spiritual forces of evil in the heavenly realms.

I thought, "Wow ... is this what is going on now with my family?" As I continued to read the Bible (and this habit is a very important key in the life of a true believer in Jesus), I began to understand the author of spiritual warfare was Satan ... the Devil.

Recorded in John 10:10 (NIV), the Apostle John tells us:

> 10 The thief (Satan) comes only to steal and kill and destroy (mankind ... including believers); I (Jesus) have come that they may have life and have it to the full.

Someone was determined to try and destroy me and my family.

I began to see and understand what's "un-praiseworthy" in this family crisis ... and I was feeling anxious and lost in my ability to control this situation.

Meditate on Praiseworthy

What was becoming very clear to me was that we live in a fallen world, full of sin and brokenness from the time of Adam, and that there's a battle going on for our souls ... a battle between good and evil.

Priscilla Shirer in her book, **The Armor of God** says, "Everything that occurs in the visible, physical world is directly connected to the wrestling match being waged in the invisible, spiritual world. The effects of the war going on in the unseen world reveal themselves in our strained and damaged relationships, emotional instability, mental fatigue, physical exhaustion, and many other areas of life ..."

This idea of spiritual warfare was all new to me, and I needed to equip myself spiritually ... not just for this issue, but for the rest of my living days here on earth. I had two choices to understand my dilemma: do I rely on worldly counsel or the wisdom of the Bible?

Fortunately, I chose the Bible. But how would I replace the ongoing contemptable, despicable, vile, and dishonorable thoughts with the admirable, credible, awesome, worthy and deserving praiseworthy thoughts of God?

The apostle Paul tells us how:

Written in 2 Corinthians 10:5 (NIV):

> ⁵ We demolish arguments and every pretension that sets itself up against the knowledge of God and we take captive every thought to make it obedient to Christ.

The human mind is a vacuum ... it gets filled daily with either the things of this world, good or bad: "unpraiseworthy" *or* it gets filled with the "excellent and praiseworthy" thoughts of God. Taking my thoughts captive simply meant to take control over what I thought about myself and my life, and especially about what was going on in our family crisis.

I asked myself, "What is God thinking about all of this? Did this family crisis take Him by surprise? Was He in heaven wondering what His next step would be? And when He figured it out, would He then let me know?"

The Commitment

Soon I would read in the Bible that God did know what He was doing, nothing comes to Him by surprise, and He had a plan in all of this.

Meditate on Praiseworthy

See Jeremiah 29:11-13 (NASB):

> 11 "For I know the plans I have for you," declares the Lord, "plans for prosperity and not for disaster, to give you a future and a hope. 12 Then you will call upon Me and come and pray to Me, and I will listen to you. 13 And you will seek Me and find Me when you search for Me with all your heart."
> ~ New American Standard Bible®, (NASB), Copyright © 1960, 1971, 1977, 1995, 2020 by The Lockman Foundation. All rights reserved.

Well, that was assuring ... *I wasn't alone in this crisis*, but I had some work to do ... to daily search the Bible for God's answers with *all* my heart. The Bible is full of wisdom ... I needed to learn how to take God's Word and make it real in my life.

The more time I spent with God in hearing, reading, studying, memorizing, and meditating on His Word, the more the Holy Spirit began teaching me how to apply this idea of taking captive my "un-praiseworthy" thoughts and replace them with "excellent and praiseworthy" thoughts.

One of my most favorite and often quoted Bible verses on which I meditate is Proverbs 3:5-7 (NASB), [emphasis by the author]:

> ⁵ Trust in the Lord with _all_ your heart and lean _not_ on _your_ own understanding; ⁶ in _all your ways_ acknowledge Him and He will make _your_ paths straight. ⁷ Do _not_ be wise in _your_ own eyes; _fear_ the Lord and _turn away_ from evil.

I had to honestly ask myself these questions:

1. "Was I truly trusting God with _all_ my heart?"
2. "Was I leaning on _my_ understanding and trying to figure out how to handle this family crisis?"
3. "Was my habit to acknowledge God constantly throughout the day, or focus my attention on how I was going to get through this crisis?"
4. "Was my path straight, or crooked and bumpy?"
5. "Was I being wise in my own eyes?"
6. "What was I fearing: my family crisis or my God?"

These were tough questions that I could only answer and face humbly as I spent time with the Lord.

> … tough questions that I could only answer and face humbly as I spent time with the Lord.

Meditate on Praiseworthy

<u>My Personal Confession and Choice to Believe</u>

I also had to ask myself whether I truly believed what the Bible said about the truth of the "excellent and praiseworthy" facts in the Bible. My family was in crisis and at risk and it was my responsibility as their father, husband, and spiritual leader, to take the lead in this matter.

I could trust my own understanding or choose to trust God as our family walked through this path of crisis. I had already trusted Jesus with my life years earlier. I trusted that He existed, that in fact, God is who the Bible says He is, and that my trust or lack of it would radically impact my life eternally.

> ... my trust or lack of it would radically impact my life eternally.

I questioned, "Was the Bible reliable? Would I trust its promises for me and my family?"

I could pick and choose which parts of the Bible I believed to be true, but I found out that the Bible didn't give me that option.

I came to believe that by faith the Word of God is *inspired*. That God divinely influenced the human authors in such a way that what they wrote was, in fact, the very Word of God.

2 Tim. 3:16 (NIV):

> ¹⁶ All Scripture is God-breathed and is useful for teaching, rebuking, correcting and training in righteousness.

I came to believe that by faith the Word of God is *true*. Here's John 17:17 (NIV):

> ¹⁷ Sanctify them by the truth; your word is truth.

Further, I chose to believe that the Bible is the guidebook for the believer's life.

Psalm 119:105 (NIV):

> ¹⁰⁵ Your word is a lamp for my feet, a light on my path.

Key question: "How could I claim the *promises* of the Bible while ignoring the *commands* of the Bible?" That seemed totally irrational. Ultimately, God has given us free will to choose what we believe. But He has also placed His fingerprints all over His creation, and He has written an instruction manual so we could know how to live.

Meditate on Praiseworthy

Psalm 119:11 (NIV):

> ¹¹ I have hidden your word in my heart that
> I might not sin against you.

I determined to believe by faith that the Bible had given me ample evidence that could be trusted, and that if I trusted it with *all my heart*, I would have a solid foundation on which to make the wise choices in leading my family through the deep waters of the crisis.

Summary and Conclusion

How would I summarize the time that has passed since this crisis occurred many years ago? There have been many "crises" in my walk with Jesus. There have been many times when all I could do was remember what James, the half-brother of Jesus, said, recorded in James 1:2-4 (NLT):

> "Dear brothers and sisters, when troubles of any kind come your way, consider it an opportunity for great joy. For you know that when your faith is tested, your endurance has a chance to grow. So let it grow, for when your endurance is fully developed, you will be perfect and complete, needing nothing."
>
> ~ *Holy Bible*, New Living Translation, copyright © 1996, 2004, 2015 by Tyndale House Foundation. Used by permission of Tyndale House Publishers, Inc., Carol Stream, Illinois 60188. All rights reserved.

Jim Robeson

As a believer in Jesus my trials or crises were designed by God to test my faith in Jesus and to grow my endurance in what God was doing in my life...making me more like Jesus. God began a work in my life even before He made the world. See Ephesians 1:4 and 5 (NIV):

> [4] For he chose us in him before the creation of the world to be holy and blameless in his sight. In love [5] he predestined us for adoption to sonship through Jesus Christ, in accordance with his pleasure and will—

and my responsibility is to trust Him with my life and walk and be led by his Spirit daily.

Please see Hebrews 11:6 (AMP):

> But without faith it is impossible to [walk with God and] please Him, for whoever comes [near] to God must [necessarily] believe that God exists and that He rewards those who [earnestly and diligently] seek Him."
> ~ **Amplified Bible** (AMP)
> Copyright © 2015 by The Lockman Foundation, La Habra, CA 90631. All rights reserved.

Meditate on Praiseworthy

God's plan for me has always been for my good, because He is a good, good God.

Please note Jeremiah 29:11 (NIV):

> ¹¹ "For I know the plans I have for you," declares the LORD, "plans to prosper you and not to harm you, plans to give you hope and a future."

And see Romans 8:28 and 29 (GW):

> ²⁸ We know that all things work together for the good of those who love God—those whom he has called according to his plan. ²⁹ This is true because he already knew his people and had already appointed them to have the same form as the image of his Son. Therefore, his Son is the firstborn among many children.
> ~**GOD'S WORD Translation** (GW)
> Copyright © 1995, 2003, 2013, 2014, 2019, 2020 by God's Word to the Nations Mission Society. All rights reserved.

Jim Robeson

Each day as I meet with the Lord and read His Word and respond in prayer, I ask Him what He wants from me and what does it mean to reflect His 'praiseworthiness?' In the quietness of the moment, I hear these words from Micah 6:8 [TLB] whispered in my ears:

> "No, he has told you what he wants, and this is all it is: to be fair, just, merciful, and to walk humbly with your God."
> ~ The Living Bible (TLB), copyright © 1971 by Tyndale House Foundation. Used by permission of Tyndale House Publishers Inc., Carol Stream, Illinois 60188. All rights reserved.

*****

Diana and Jim Robeson, Photograph by Jim Robeson, July, 2019 * California Coast, Northern California

How Jim Robeson and Glen Aubrey became acquainted:

From Jim:

I first met Glen in 2006 when he was hired by our small church in San Diego, California: Community Bible Church under the original leadership of Dr. Gene French. At that time, our church's growth was exceeding the staff's ability to "equip the saints for the work of the ministry."

Glen's purpose was to first coach our staff in establishing a solid spiritual foundation in our own lives before we could do the same for our congregation. He would later build on that foundation by helping us understand some best practices for growing churches. At that time, I had very little experience in leading a church staff as an Executive Pastor. So right away Glen had my undivided attention.

What I came to find out was that this wasn't Glen's first rodeo, so to speak. His resume included working with major businesses and churches across the nation.

Our time together wasn't for just a few weeks. We had contracted Glen for almost a year, and it took that long to gain everyone's respect and commitment. It was a bumpy road early on for sure.

As I remember, some of the staff didn't stay around for long and we ended up "cleaning house" and hiring those who wanted to work as a "team" ... not those who "knew it all" and could only work alone.

I am so thankful that the Lord brought Glen into my life. There are so many life principles that I have learned from Glen over the years and that I use daily.

Let me say one final thing about my relationship with Glen that I carry with me today. One of my favorite verses in the Bible that describes my relationship with Glen is this:

> "You have heard me teach things that have been confirmed by many reliable witnesses. Now teach these truths to other trustworthy people who will be able to pass them on to others."
> 2 Timothy 2:2 NLT
> ~ *Holy Bible*, New Living Translation, copyright © 1996, 2004, 2015 by Tyndale House Foundation. Used by permission of Tyndale House Publishers, Inc., Carol Stream, Illinois 60188. All rights reserved.

My questions to you who are reading this chapter are these:

1. "Who is mentoring you as you walk along your life path?
2. To whom are you passing those important life skills that you are learning?"

The result of passing on what you are learning is "real life" and true *joy*!

~ Jim Robeson President and CEO;
Chartered Life Underwriter, Chartered Financial Consultant; Robeson and Associates, Inc. DBA
The Medicare Answer Guy
May, 2022

<u>From Glen</u>:

The first time I met Jim Robeson I believed I was entering into an acquaintance with a dedicated and Christ-centered man. That first impression belief has proven solidly true over time. Jim has become a true, giving, and reliable friend.

My task at the church was to consult with leadership, staff, and volunteers. The goal of a church "consultant" in those days was, in my language, to "work myself out of a job" by training a team of individuals who would provide the church and its ministries with communication outreach in Programming Arts, consisting of: <u>music</u> (vocal and instrumental), <u>media</u> (what is "seen" including but not limited to video, visual imagery, banners), <u>drama</u> (vignettes and/or more full length presentations), <u>technical services</u> (sound and lights), <u>support services</u> (ushering and parking lot assistance), <u>administration</u> (office staff, communication), <u>stage design</u>, and <u>artistic direction</u>.

Jim and I served this church at a time of unique development and growth. It was thrilling to see the church expand its ministries as time went on. Of course, challenge, change, conflict, and renewed communication were all part of the mix. It was not necessarily a bumpy-free road; ministry never is, nor is it expected to be. But it was a God-centered effort. Jim was an influential and vital aspect of its success. I treasure Jim's and my relationship. Perhaps one of the comments I will add is this one: you can trust him. That is refreshing today and every day.

~ Glen Aubrey
May, 2022

Chapter Nine
Think About Such Things

By Glen Aubrey

When we "think about such things," we should prayerfully and personally codify (classify) our thoughts into a form that may be more easily understood, practical, and that follows our understanding of the Bible. We don't write new truth; rather, we endeavor to state God's existing truth in ways easy to understand and apply.

One item to keep in mind: the Bible builds upon God's eternal life-giving truth, starting with Genesis 1:1, "In the beginning God created the heavens and the earth." Further, the Bible has been proven historically accurate, and is primarily written for our redemption. To accomplish codification, through our parent organization, Creative Team Resources Group LLC (CTRG), we created documents which together formed the foundation of our purpose, principles, and practices.

The first one is Values, Vision, Mission, and Message. This document deals with essential human interactions and offers governing guidance for an individual, group, or team.

Ideally, all agree on what they believe, why they exist, their primary purpose (what they are called to accomplish), and the background truth they wish to teach others.

*****

Values, Vision, Mission, and Message

Values: the principles upon which we agree

Vision: the reasons why our organization or team exists

Mission: our actions in fulfillment of values and vision

Message: the lessons we learn, model, and teach to the people we are called to reach

An effective way to begin the codification process may be to ask questions of each member of the group. These can be questions like these, below:

VALUES:

What do we value most in our leaders and followers?

Answers usually include these high, moral, and righteous characteristics. A brief definition follows each category:

a. <u>Honesty and Integrity</u>: truth, trustworthiness, and reliability in word and deed
b. <u>Authenticity</u>: words and deeds that match
c. <u>Relationships</u>: decisions and choices about another's success
d. <u>Functional Excellence</u>: proofs of the effectiveness of our relationships
e. <u>Modeling</u>: duplication into others' lives
f. <u>Legacy</u>: greater works from our followers
g. <u>Accountability</u>: completion and closure
h. <u>Enjoyment</u>: celebration of people and process
i. <u>Rewards</u>: intangible and tangible results of our efforts
j. <u>Experience</u>: full engagement on the journey of growth

VISION:

To see lives and organizations changed for the better

MISSION:

We provide great information that encourages people to make better decisions and choices about how they live and work, and we do this through building Core Teams.

MESSAGE:

People are more important than what they do.

Glen Aubrey

The Four Questions

We created **The Four Questions** to more fully explain Values, Vision, Mission, and Message.

1. **Who are you at your core?**

    *This is a question of **values**.* This question seeks to know the heart-core of the individuals, what makes them tick, what are their principled, unchangeable, bedrock beliefs upon which their entire world-view and actions are based. In a trustworthy candidate, these values will likely include but not be limited to intangibles of integrity, trust, commitment, faithfulness, respect, cooperation and love.

2. **What are you called to accomplish?**

    *This is a question of **vision**.* Vision gives purpose. Where this question is answered with a list of tangibles, the candidate is veering off course. Accomplishments are heart-related when they seek to build up other people and accomplish goals through investment. Vision is best described in intangibles. If a candidate refers to benefits seen in values as opposed to benefits seen in valuables, the question and answer are hitting home.

3. **What do you want?**

*This is a question of **mission***. Missions are actions to fulfill a goal, and their accomplishment is seen in their effects, both materially and within a frame of mind. What a follower wants should be in direct correlation to the answers to the first two questions. The mission will include hard work and the satisfaction coming from completing a job well. Happiness should be evidenced in tangible rewards—the products of achievement—along with intangible inner repose— an assurance of attainment, a healthy sense of pride in the fulfillment of purpose.

4. **Whom will you impact?**

*This is a question of **message***. Lessons learned are worth little until they become operative in real life. People long for and appreciate authenticity when actions verify words. People who are impacted for good because of a follower's or leader's life model can find themselves in a state of receptivity for learning what, how, and why something or someone worked. Principled truth that invades and transforms life makes people take notice, and for those who desire more than mediocrity, creates hungers for more of whatever "that" is and wherever "it" came from. Message is seen through measures and methods. Message is enfolded into desires, decisions and deeds.

The life-lessons learned and taught to those who observe and want to receive them, become the message.

*****

The CORE TEAM

The term CORE TEAM was first introduced in the statement of Mission:

We provide great information that encourages people to make better decisions and choices about how they live and work, and
we do this through building Core Teams.

The Core Team is an organizational entity used to personalize and activate Values, Vision, Mission, and Message. The description of a CORE TEAM is in spelling as well as chronological order:

C – **Consistency**: faithfulness demonstrated in words, and actions

O – **Obedience:** to our agreed values

R – **Right Relationships:** (what we call decisions and choices about others' success: while we cannot "own" someone else's success, we can create environments that promote success)

E – **Example**: the question is never *if* we have an example; it's always what *kind* of an example do we have

T – **Trust**: essentially there are three kinds: the first is <u>unearned</u>, usually granted at the beginning of every relationship; the second is <u>validated</u>, verified over time and shared experiences; the third is <u>violated</u> which is a disruption of assured reliance placed in another's words or actions; to <u>re-establish trust</u> in a relationship, start with an understanding that we must grant something again that has not been earned, yet.

E – **Essentials of Your Composite Nature**:
a) Experience (unique to you)
b) Education (unlimited, and up to each individual to pursue)
c) Environment (you and I choose the environment we create every day; whether conditions are ill-favored or not, we still must and do choose how we deal with them, in attitude, approach, and action)

A – **Accountability**: how do you strive for accountability in words and deeds?

M – **Method**: Your choice of method (what you do and how you do it) is, and always will be a direct result of how much the relational concepts that make up C, O, R, E -- T, E, A are fully agreed upon and activated. C, O, R, E -- T, E, A are relationally based concepts/creeds/truths. All precede action. Action is method. Method again, is what you do and how you do it.

Core Team Chart

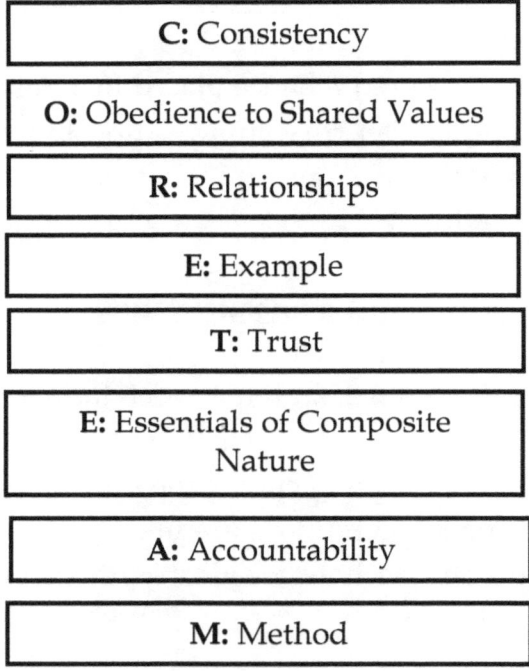

*****

Finally, I want to offer you what we call **A Value System**. It is a culmination of *personal action commitments* which are direct results of applying what you have just read.

Its title is **The Twelve Laws of Understanding**. The term "Understanding" means first and foremost understanding us—from the inside out. The more we understand our personal responsibilities, the more we codify our commitments and activate them, following God's leading.

A Value System

The Twelve Laws of Understanding

1. Realize I am responsible for my own choices, not others'; that changing someone else's behavior is not my responsibility; rather, I need to change me.
2. Seek to understand how the other person thinks and communicates; use his or her language.
3. Model what I want.
4. Set realistic limits on what is acceptable behavior.
5. Impose these limits on myself, first.
6. Desire the best, but prepare for difficulty; seek creative, peaceful solutions.
7. Seek and pray for wisdom.
8. Remember, at the right times.
9. Encourage always.
10. Think first, listen most, and speak seldom.
11. Realize growth involves change, change can mean pain, and patience on the journey is a virtue.
12. Love. Establish meaningful relationships.

*****

Chapter Ten
Attributes, Attitudes, and Actions

By Glen Aubrey

The Attributes of Philippians 4:8 are presented as guideposts for us, instructing us how to live. They are followed by the personal choices of Attitudes, and result in the Actions we choose.

Here is Paul's list again. Each word begins with the phrase "Whatever is …"

1. True
2. Noble
3. Right
4. Pure
5. Lovely
6. Admirable
7. Excellent
8. Praiseworthy

<u>Think about such things</u>.

Yes, we are told how to think. This admonition is for our good.

Paul knew the inherent value of convincing in the mind. Dwelling on these attributes helps direct and realign our thinking into the mind of the Lord, for how we conduct our lives. This might be fairly easy to understand, but sometimes hard to put into practice recurringly. Our realistic goal is *not* perfection (it can't be); rather, our goal is to live with these thoughts and through them let God direct our actions. <u>Our desire is to obey as a true reflection of our commitments</u>.

Following God begins with an Attitude of desire to submit to God's leading without reservation. Attitudes precede and guide Actions.

Consider: when we don't follow this list, we run the real risk of not doing well, because we are not dedicated enough to first possess the mental assent of the truth of the passage, and second, the activities which must follow when attitudes are aligned with God's will.

AAA Diagram

Perhaps a simple chart may offer further clarity. This graphic is of a three-legged stool. We've all seen them, and likely have utilized them, too. Each leg supports the whole; therefore, each leg is vital to the structural integrity of the support provided by the stool.

Attributes, Attitudes, and Actions

Let's call this The Diagram of Support of a Believer's Life Practices.

Each leg is labeled, as follows:

Attributes
        Attitudes
                Actions

The Diagram of Support of a Believer's Life Practices

Attributes   **Attitudes**   **Actions**

Each leg is necessary for the structural integrity of the whole. Without each leg performing its duty, the stool can topple over.

Here's an illustration: Acceptance of the Attributes and Attitudes *without* Actions may be what James had in mind when he wrote these words, recorded for us in James 2:13-17 (author emphasis):

> "[14] What good is it, my brothers and sisters, if someone claims to have faith but has no deeds? Can such faith save them? [15] Suppose a brother or a sister is without clothes and daily food. [16] If one of you says to them, "Go in peace; keep warm and well fed," but does nothing about their physical needs, what good is it? [17] In the same way, *faith by itself, if it is not accompanied by action, is dead.*"

We can talk faith, but let's walk it, too. "Talk and Walk" belong together.

Further, a desire to **do** the right things without understanding a more complete intent of these Attributes and Attitudes, may mean: though actions are performed, they may not originate from the most complete understanding of ***what*** to do and ***how best*** to do it, to provide a *true* benefit to the receiver.

Attributes, Attitudes, and Actions

For example, a huge difference exists between a handout, and a hand up. Simply, providing a **handout** without knowing what exactly is behind a need, without allowing for an opportunity for growth, even discouraging development, may foster enablement and dependence. Enabling is never wise. Have you known of someone who, through acquiring more complete understanding, your encouragement, along with personal desire and willpower, may grasp the opportunity to grow and mature when it is shown that he/she truly desires owning personal responsibility? This person may simply need assistance to get going again.

The Apostle Paul in 2 Thessalonians 3:10 describes his understanding and instruction of personal responsibility quite clearly when he says this:

> 10 For even when we were with you, we gave you this rule: "The one who is unwilling to work shall not eat."

The descriptive word is "unwilling." It implies that one in this state refuses ownership of responsibility for his or her own welfare.

In strong contrast, a **hand up** is a strong example of providing for the needs of one where, apart from that provision, a need goes unmet.

Remember our quoted verse in James 1:27, and the author's description of "true" religion: it is *first* meeting needs of orphans and people in distress:

> Religion that God our Father accepts as **pure and faultless** is this: to look after orphans and widows in their distress and to keep oneself from being polluted by the world."

An orphan is described by Merriam-Webster as "one deprived, (as a child for example who has lost his or her parents), of protection or advantage." This person may not be able to help themselves. Such is or can be true also with widows, "in distress." This could be from difficulties physically, mentally, or in light of loss. "Distress" is defined as: "trouble" or "misfortune", "a state of danger or desperate need" from Merriam-Webster. That's clear enough.

A very close relative of mine spent several months caring for her mother when she suffered from dementia, and eventually she required care from hospice. The outpouring of love demonstrated to her own mother by this relative, was love from the heart. And mom was grateful, too!

Those circumstances reminded me that many years ago I had offered to take care of my step grandfather after he had turned 90 and had quit driving (thankfully—the stopping driving was a relief). My taking care of him meant grocery shopping at least twice a week, going to his home almost daily

Attributes, Attitudes, and Actions

to check up on him, taking him to lunch, and providing for other needs. Did it take my time? Yes, but on the death of my grandmother who had passed earlier, I asked him if he wanted my help, to which he replied, "Yes." It was my honor to take care of him until the Lord took him.

He was a WW I Veteran, having served in France in the Medical Corps during that conflict. Later, he was employed at Pearl Harbor (Hickam Field) as a civilian contractor when, on December 7, 1941, the base was bombed by the Japanese, which ushered in our declaration of war with Japan.

Oh, the stories he would tell, about the Pearl Harbor attack that day! Of course, he was an eye-witness to the carnage. I couldn't hear his first-hand tales often enough! I miss him and his retelling of history yet today.

Now moving to the topic of gifts presented from less than an upright spirit, let's inquire: have you ever known of a gift not given from a right attitude? Have you ever received a gift from someone whose attitude had proven less than a true spirit of blessing?

In cases where giving is not accomplished with a right attitude and intent to bless, it may be far less than "giving;" indeed, it could be manipulation for selfish gain. A gift given with wrong motives can be a prelude for stealing, misappropriation of funds, lying, and less than honest actions.

I have been on the receiving end of this kind of mis-aligned gifting, and fortunately was able to shut it down before lasting misunderstandings and trouble ensued. The transactions proposed didn't seem right, from the very beginning from one individual. The experience of others who dealt with him proved the misgivings correct. It was more than sad and soul disappointing.

Summary: a right attitude is vital to assure that attributes of quality and right character are not sacrificed on an altar of greed.

> ... a right attitude is vital to assure that attributes of quality and right character are not sacrificed on an altar of greed.

How important are all three legs of this believer's stool of life practices? Each one is completely necessary for the Attributes of giving, sharing, compassion, and love to be fulfilled with Godly motives seen in righteous attitudes and effective actions.

*****

Chapter Eleven
Choices

By Glen Aubrey

Our Creative Team Publishing author, John Emra, with his wife, Sheryl, has spoken consistently for nearly as long as we have known each other, about the *difference* between decision and choice. His truths resonate with me for these reasons:

1. They are true.
2. They are profound.
3. Correctly applied, they improve and positively alter environments and results through changed lives.

John Emra specifically states, "We all make choices every day and choices have consequences. The difference between choice and decision *is* the consequence."

John's books deal with this difference and associated results at length. Although directed at parents, these truths are for any age and circumstance.

His books:

1. *Cornerstones and Core Needs of Growing Kids*
2. *Parenting from the Top of the Mountain*
3. *Seven Steps to the Top of the Mountain*

John Emra's website: **www.lifeisfullofchoices.org**

Using Merriam-Webster for a related perspective:

1. Decision: a determination arrived at after consideration : Conclusion
2. Choice: selection; the power of selecting an option

One difference readily apparent is that decision is a conclusion or determination that may or may not include an associated action. On the contrary, choice is all about selecting an option and acting upon it. And that choice does have consequences!

In fact, God's choice has eternal consequences for us, and He modeled this best when He chose us for adoption as sons and daughters. In Ephesians 1:3-10 (emphasis mine), it says:

> [3] Blessed be the God and Father of our Lord Jesus Christ, who has blessed us in Christ with every spiritual blessing in the

heavenly places, 4 even as HE CHOSE US in him before the foundation of the world, that we should be holy and blameless before him. In love 5 he predestined us for adoption to himself as sons through Jesus Christ, according to the purpose of his will, 6 to the praise of his glorious grace, with which he has blessed us in the Beloved. 7 In him we have redemption through his blood, the forgiveness of our trespasses, according to the riches of his grace, 8 which he lavished upon us, in all wisdom and insight 9 making known to us the mystery of his will, according to his purpose, which he set forth in Christ 10 as a plan for the fullness of time, to unite all things in him, things in heaven and things on earth.

~ The Holy Bible, English Standard Version. ESV® Text Edition: 2016. Copyright © 2001 by Crossway Bibles, a publishing ministry of Good News Publishers.

When you and I *choose* faith, we *choose* to believe and trust God. This choice of belief is by God's grace and ushers in redemption for us, and then is proven to others by our works, hopefully mirroring God's work in us.

Indeed, the doorway to faith is based on God's love and grace, never our meritorious actions, or so-called worth. There is nothing we can do to merit salvation. This act of redemption before God is achieved only from receiving "by grace through faith." (according to Ephesians 2:8)

But faith, when it is active, is seen and evidenced by works of service, proven by actions, not just a decision for Christ. Rather, it's a choice evidenced in living activities.

According to the book of James, "Faith without works is dead, being alone." More specifically, James 2: 14-18 (NIV):

> [14] What good is it, my brothers and sisters, if someone claims to have faith but has no deeds? Can such faith save them? [15] Suppose a brother or a sister is without clothes and daily food. [16] If one of you says to them, "Go in peace; keep warm and well fed," but does nothing about their physical needs, what good is it? [17] In the same way, faith by itself, if it is not accompanied by action, is dead. [18] But someone will say, "You have faith; I have deeds." Show me your faith

Choices

without deeds, and I will show you my
faith by my deeds.

The value of choice is unquestioned. In the process of choosing holistic health, we are confronted with the opportunity to choose these options:

1. **Holistic Health**: a book I highly recommend is written by Rick Redd, MD. Having read and applying it, I have seen marked improvements in my health over the last three years (2019 – 2022). Title: ***All-In Or Nothing Beyond Retirement*** for anyone over age 50. If younger, ***All-In Or Nothing * Master Your Destiny***. Website: www.all-inornothing.com

2. **Holistic Faith**: I am a believer in, and follower of, Christ. I encourage acquisition and reading of the following books, among thousands from which to choose. These are books of faith and inspiration which are, and have been, important in my life and study:

    a. *The Holy Bible*, New International Version (NIV)
    b. ***God's Plan Unfolding * Strength and Renewal in Times of Crisis*** by Glen Aubrey www.godsplanunfolding.com

c. ***God's Promises * Every One Fulfilled*** by Glen Aubrey
www.godspromisesfulfilled.com
d. ***The Word Became Flesh*** by E. Stanley Jones
e. ***Doctor Hudson's Secret Journal*** by Lloyd C. Douglas
f. ***Lord of the Rings*** by J. R. R. Tolkien
g. ***A Little Book about Prayer*** by W. E. McCumber
h. ***Resilient Warriors*** by Robert F. Dees
www.resiliencetrilogy.com
i. ***Resilient Warriors Advanced Study Guide***
www.resiliencetrilogy.com
j. ***Resilient Leaders*** by Robert F. Dees
www.resiliencetrilogy.com
k. ***Resilient Nations*** by Robert F. Dees
www.resiliencetrilogy.com
l. ***Resilience God Style*** by Robert F. Dees
www.resiliencegodstyle.com
m. ***Resilience God Style Study Guide***
www.resiliencegodstyle.com
n. ***Riding the Fence Really Hurts! * Embrace God's Plan for Your Life*** by Judy Bowen (available on Amazon)
o. ***Faith Matters * The Breakthrough You Want*** by Glen Aubrey
www.faithmatterstoyou.com
p. ***Extreme Investing * Changing the World One Believer at a Time*** by Barry Willey

q. ***Out of the Valley * An Amazing Life Story that Can Help You Make Good Choices ... and Leave an Eternal Destiny*** by Barry Willey
r. ***What If God Is Like This? * Meet the God You've Never Known*** by Will Hathaway
http://www.will-hathaway.com/
s. ***The Human Side of Christ * Meet the Guy Behind the God*** by Will Hathaway
http://www.will-hathaway.com/
t. ***Naked*** by Will Hathaway
http://www.will-hathaway.com/
u. ***Knowing You Have Done Your Best * No Regrets*** by Angela Williams
www.knowingyouhavedoneyourbest.com
v. ***Finding God in Silicon Valley*** by Skip Vaccarello
www.skipvaccarello.com
w. ***Enjoy Greater Results with Less Effort * Build a Better You*** by Bud Hendrickson
www.greaterresultslesseffort.com
x. ***Forgive Especially When It Doesn't Make Sense*** by Debi McNamer (available on Amazon)
y. ***The Addict's Choices * From Depths of Isolation to Heights of True Forgiveness*** by John Wesley Childress
www.lifeisfullofchoices.org

z. *Grief Is Not the End* by Bill Trask
   https://hopeandloss.com/
aa. *The Robe* by Lloyd C. Douglass

3. **Holistic Leadership in Business and Personally**:

True, morally anchored, honest, Christ-honoring, effective leadership is evidenced when a leader genuinely serves those who follow him or her. Holistic leaders start their journey of servant leadership as faithful followers long before they lead.

Faithful followers are not born as leaders. In reverence and submission, they grow into lasting leadership by willingly adopting Christ's model of serving long before they ever ascend to leadership of others.

They lead in the model of Christ; there is no other way.

Remember this verse? Mark 9:35 (NIV):

Sitting down, Jesus called the Twelve and said, "Anyone who wants to be first must be the very last, and the servant of all."

Choices

What is the call and desire for authentic humility before God? Humility, again from Merriam-Webster, is defined as: "freedom *from* pride or arrogance." (Author emphasis) Notice this definition is couched in the phrase "freedom from" pride, arrogance, or self-serving attitudes and actions. This is not freedom *to* exercise humility.

Humility begins by knowing what we are called to give up and surrender.

4. **<u>Holistic Approach to Challenges</u>**:

From an original song, written in the 1970s, and presented by The Revelaires Quartet:

"It's a challenge to live the right kind of life
In a world like ours today.
It's a challenge to let them know where you stand
When you're walking the Christian way:

A challenge that can only be met with power,
And there's power in the Son of God.
Never run away from the challenge, my friend.
Be strong and meet the challenge head-on!" ~ Glen Aubrey

It was a catchy tune, "fun" in execution, and the lyrics carried immense weight in meaning.

How do we face challenges now, knowing they may reveal themselves in all kinds of ways? Consider these Biblically-based responses:

1. Immediately forgive those who may present or even represent challenges to you, especially if you believe you have been offended in any way.
2. Yearn to see God's hand in everything that transpires.
3. Request that God teach you His lessons your challenges include.
4. Model His teaching for others.
5. Give struggles to God; remain faithful to trust Him in all of them. Obey His commands.
6. Pray for a God-driven and God-glorifying outcome for every challenge, including prayer for any individuals who are responsible for any of them.
7. Seek peace as you request and pray for God's wisdom in facing all problems.

Choices

When facing a test or challenge, let's inquire:

<u>Question</u>: is it true that God will be our *greatest* Helper in challenges we may encounter?

<u>Answer</u>: unequivocally yes!

5. **Holistic Demeanor:**

   Faith and belief cannot be hidden if true; wear them and share them.

   "Demeanor" is outwardly observed behaviors, especially toward others.

   Let people around you observe your faith because it is in plain view. Let the content of what is observed match the inner faith God has given you.

6. **Holistic Character and Attributes:**

   Character grows internally long before it manifests itself externally. It is never hidden, at least for long. It always reveals itself.

   The attributes of Philippians 4:8 work from the inside out. When embraced, God uses these attributes to further sanctify a person.

Excellence:

God desires our best; He gave us His.

Since excellence is what we observe in Him, can we do any less than give Him our all, striving to fulfill His call and design for our lives?

7. **Holistic Perseverance:**

My dear friend, Dave Hopkins, wrote a captivating melody for the NIV version of James 1:2:

"Consider it pure joy, my brothers, whenever you face trials of many kinds; Consider it pure joy my brothers, because you know that the testing of your faith develops perseverance."

In this song and the scriptures it employs as lyrics, perseverance is a word used to indicate "staying power." Perseverance is the lasting quality of holding on to truth, knowing truth lasts beyond any temporal trials. It is defined as those circumstances or events related to time as opposed to eternity.

Occurrences and circumstances are temporary. Perseverance remains. It stays true throughout this life. Its eternal effects become evident in the next. It lasts. It never lets go, and never gives up.

8. **<u>Holistic Joy:</u>**

I recall my parents singing an old Gospel song when I was just a young boy. It was composed by Barney Elliott Warren in 1900. It is, therefore, in the public domain.

From Hymnary.org

(1) I have found His grace is all complete;
He supplieth every need.
While I sit and learn at Jesus' feet,
I am free, yes, free indeed.

<u>Refrain</u>:

It is joy unspeakable and full of glory,
Full of glory, full of glory.
It is joy unspeakable and full of glory;
O the half has never yet been told!

(2) I have found the pleasure I once craved;
It is joy and peace within.
What a wondrous blessing! I am saved
From the awful gulf of sin. [Refrain]

(3) I have found that hope so bright and
    clear,
Living in the realm of grace.
O the Savior's presence is so near;
I can see his smiling face. [Refrain]

(4) I have found the joy no tongue can
    tell,
How its waves of glory roll!
It is like a great o'erflowing well,
Springing up within my soul. [Refrain]

How do we possess God's holistic and unspeakable joy?

Far more than an emotion only, this joy is a deep, inward satisfaction bathed in God's peace and assurance because of what He has given to us, done for us, promises to us, and guarantees on our behalf. It's a part of our relationship with Him.

Surpassing emotion, though it may include emotional responses, this joy is inward satisfaction, *regardless of circumstances*, resting in Who God is, and all He has provided in Christ.

Note that "joy" is an encouraged response for us to employ. It is a "consideration" of ours when trials are to be faced. "Consider it pure joy, my brothers, whenever you face trials of many kinds." Perhaps heaven-birthed joy is best realized in the midst of negative occurrences and difficult times.

Another item that comes to mind is my own interpretation of "joy" as a part of the story of Christ, His purpose and plan.

Recall this verse in the King James Version. It's found in **Hebrews 12:2** (author emphasis):

² Looking unto Jesus the author and finisher of our faith; who <u>for the joy that was set before him</u> endured the **<u>cross</u>**, despising the **<u>shame</u>**, and is set down at the right hand of the throne of God.

I have often said that the "joy that was set before Him," was His ultimate victory for us. He reigns over us, as King of Kings and Lord of Lords. We, and all those who believe and receive Him, are the reasons He came, died, and rose again in a final victory over death, sin, hell, and the grave. How could His cross and shame be described as "joy?" I believe this is true only because the positive ending was promised and guaranteed before the crucifixion was begun. The cross never minimized the pain of sacrifice;

the promise of "joy" was, however, the reason He was able to endure. His triumph became and is our guarantee of overcoming through His power.

9. **Holistic Reality:**

Reality is defined as: "the quality or state of being real; something that is neither derivative nor dependent but exists necessarily" ~Merriam-Webster.

Holistic reality is wholeness of the complete body, mind, soul, and spirit. Nothing is overlooked, discarded, or left out. Holistic reality is all-inclusive to the creation of humankind. Our holistic reality is discovered and made true in the centrality and kingship, or lordship, of Jesus.

*****

Let's inquire: what is our response to the invitation to "Return to Holistic Health?" A full and unfettered alignment with the cause, sacrifice, and victory of Christ is the necessary option for us all. But we must choose.

Choices

This alignment begins with His calling, and is consummated in our acceptance of, and obedience to Him.

The old hymn **Trust and Obey** sums it up well. The Lyrics were written by John Henry Sammis (1846-1919) and the Music was composed by Daniel Brink Towner (1850-1919). This song is in the public domain.

> (1) When we walk with the Lord
> In the light of His Word,
> What a glory He sheds on our way;
> While we do His good will,
> He abides with us still,
> And with all who will trust and obey.
>
> [Refrain:]
> Trust and obey,
> For there's no other way
> To be happy in Jesus,
> But to trust and obey.
>
> (2) Not a shadow can rise,
> Not a cloud in the skies,
> But His smile quickly drives it away,
> Not a doubt or a fear,
> Not a sigh or tear,

Glen Aubrey

Can abide while we trust and obey.
[Refrain]

(3) Not a burden we bear,
Nor a sorrow we share,
But our toil He doth richly repay;
Not a grief or a loss,
Not a frown or a cross,
But is blest if we trust and obey.
[Refrain]

(4) But we never can prove
The delights of His love,
Until all on the altar we lay;
For the favor He shows,
And the joy He bestows,
Are for them who will trust and
obey. [Refrain]

(5) Then in fellowship sweet
We will sit at His feet,
Or we'll walk by His side in the way;
What He says we will do;
Where He sends, we will go,
Never fear, only trust and obey.
[Refrain]

Choices

How willing are we to submit to God's leading, His will, and then trust and obey without reservation? The answer to that question assures our destiny.

*****

Gather The Children

Glen Aubrey

In 1975 I was blessed to compose *Gather The Children*. This song and its lyrics are uniquely tied to a central theme of this book: illustrating the profound truth of God's love ***through us*** to touch all those in our spheres of influence, and beyond.

The piece was composed to answer a call to engage in outreach, and as an encouragement to all of us to express God's love. This is our central focus for life.

The lyrics are presented first. They are followed with a scan of the original music score.

(1) "Lift up your eyes, and look on the fields,
For they are white already to harvest."
The field is the world, and we are the sowers,
Sent to share the Good News of Jesus.

Gather the Children, all the lost children,
See them and reach them with God's precious love.
Lives that are broken, alone, and forgotten
Jesus remembers and loves them through us.

Gather The Children

(2) The Great Commission says, "Go into the world,
And preach the gospel to ev'ry creature."
With love to light our way, and His strength sustaining,
We go forth to tell the world of Jesus.

Gather the Children, all the lost children,
See them and reach them with God's precious love.
Lives that are broken, alone, and forgotten
Jesus remembers and loves them through us.

(3) Our world is vast, and needs love so much!
It is for us to share to share God's love to reach them.
People need to see our Savior's compassion
In the lives of all those who follow Him.

Gather the Children, all the lost children,
See them and reach them with God's precious love.
Lives that are broken, alone, and forgotten
Jesus remembers and loves them through us.

Lives that are broken, alone, and forgotten
Jesus remembers and loves them through us.
Jesus remembers and loves them through us.

*****

Here is a scan of the original score.

Gather The Children

Gather The Children

Gather The Children

Chapter Twelve
Transformation, Change, and A New Direction

By Rick Redd, MD

I became a physician many years ago because I wanted to be a part of one of the noblest professions on earth. I wanted to help people be their healthiest, so that they could live vital, productive lives and exercise their God-given talents to the maximum. Health is the foundation upon which success is built. I wanted to imagine a world where the majority of people were enjoying fulfilled lives.

I was educated, trained, and inspired for nine years after college by some of the best medical professionals in the world, and I was at the top of my "game" when I started to practice in radiology in 1981.

In the 70s and early 80s, the emphasis in medical school, internship, and residency was finding out what was "wrong" with the patient by taking a history of the present illness, conducting a review of the body's systems (respiratory, gastrointestinal, endocrine, and so forth), and performing a complete physical examination.

Rick Redd, MD

My most coveted possessions:

1. A state-of-the-art stethoscope
2. A battery-operated otoscope/ophthalmoscope.

We had a substantial number of lab tests from which to choose in trying to narrow our differential diagnosis, but the objective was to be as judicious as possible in the choice of those tests. Even if the test was available at our hospital, the cost to the patient was always a significant restrictive factor. Doing a large number of tests on any one patient was considered boorish and profoundly unnecessary.

Diagnostic radiology in the early 80s was limited to x-rays, fluoroscopy, nuclear medicine, ultrasound, and a limited number of special procedures (arthroscopy for joint evaluation, myelography for the spine, and angiography to further define the arteries and veins). Computed tomography (CT) had just been developed, but there were no multi-slice scanners. MRI, PET-CT, and interventional radiology were non-existent.

It was a simpler time, then, more reasonable and more balanced. We still felt like we were practicing excellent medicine; we were performing as well as the art and the science would take us. Technology was still in its infancy, but we had no idea how to gauge its impact or how to anticipate what was yet to come.

Transformation, Change, and A New Direction

The computer was just being developed, and its importance to medicine and to society in general had not yet been fully realized. Real-time ultrasound was the newest and most innovative diagnostic tool available, requiring new skill sets for the radiologists and a broader knowledge base. It was just the beginning of what was to come.

What none of us realized at the time, was just how quickly information was being generated and gathered. I vividly remember listening to our commencement speaker at Oregon Health Sciences University in 1976, as he told us that the faculty had vigorously tried to present current data to us throughout our years of training, and that still "half of the material you now possess is outdated." "Your task," he said, "is to figure out which half is still valid for your patients." I realized that day that life-long learning had become a way of life if one hoped to stay current with the art and science of medicine.

It is difficult to know when United States medicine began its slow decline into professional mediocrity, and patients began to become dissatisfied with the quality of care they were receiving.

Four megatrends occurred over the years which changed medicine substantively, and *not* always for the better:

1. Diagnostic imaging continued to ride the wave of innovation as computed tomography, magnetic

resonance imaging, positron-emission tomography and interventional radiology came into their own. Using Quantum Field Theory was foundational in bringing this technology into play. Human anatomy and physiology were being understood and displayed better than ever before in history. But while the imaging field was growing, most of medicine was not.

2. Even after billions of Federal dollars were pumped into the vascular system of the US economy in trying to get a handle on poverty, the wars on drugs, heart disease, and cancer, little meaningful success was realized. Many of us wondered why scientific advancements in the <u>treatment</u> of disease were not being effectively utilized. What or who was holding this back? Many of us were slowly becoming disillusioned.

3. Paying for health care was pried from the clenched fists of the American public; the government became the controller of the medical dollar, and all that goes with it. Have you wondered why the cost of medical care has skyrocketed? There are three primary reasons:

    a. The American patient had no incentive to look for the best deal in spending their medical dollars wisely. We had been suckered into a system where we were spending "other people's money" instead of our own.

    b. Insurance companies enriched themselves, especially after the Affordable Care Act (Obama Care) became the law of the land.

c. Big Pharma generated thousands of new medicines to feed the public's desire for symptom relief, not cures of disease. The quick-fix mentality became preeminent.
d. The practice of medicine in the United States became very lucrative (currently 19% of our country's gross domestic product), and a source of great potential power for controlling the people. It was more than the power-brokers and the politicians could overlook. The medical-industrial complex in the United States became a six-headed hydra which collectively controlled the direction and magnitude of the way medicine was practiced. Leadership, education, research, and even medical practice itself was gradually and inexorably wrested from the hands of the medical experts (the doctors). Those six heads were:

   i. The United States government, including the legislative, executive and judicial branches, FDA, NIH, CDC-P, and others.
   ii. United States medicine, including the educational institutions, research facilities and journals, and regulatory bodies which control the administration of medicine.
   iii. Medical insurance industry
   iv. Pharmacology industry
   v. Food manufacturing and farming industry

vi. Legal industry—including medical regulations, standards of care, and malpractice suits

Over the years, I became so disenchanted with how medicine was evolving and the poor results we were getting in our country, that I strongly considered choosing another vocation. In 2011, I learned that I was not alone in my thinking, and that there was a new type of medicine taking shape. I began to relearn and retrain according to those precepts (called Integrative Medicine, because it combined the best of the Western and Eastern philosophies of medicine) at the University of Arizona in Tucson, under the tutelage of Dr Andrew Weil. This was the better way I had been searching for!

Are your thoughts about the American healthcare system similar to mine? Do you believe that United States medicine is the best in the world? Is it the most reasonably priced? Is it easy to access? Are you satisfied with the quality of care you receive on a consistent basis?

Please hear me correctly. I am *not* saying that the physicians and other care providers are not well-trained or highly motivated to care for you. Allopathic physicians are very good at what they do (acute care medicine, surgery, diagnostic imaging). What I *am* saying is that the *results* we are getting as we age are not what we deserve or should expect.

Transformation, Change, and A New Direction

The chronic diseases of aging (heart disease, strokes, cancer, inflammation, and autoimmune disease, diabetes, and obesity, and Alzheimer's dementia) are not being effectively dealt with. The "facts" about all of medicine don't support the inflated beliefs that we hold. We need better.

I am reminded of a statement which Mark Twain once said:

> I am not as worried about what I don't know, as I am about what I think I do know, which is just flatly not true.

The *truth* is that our medical system is based on a false set of beliefs, a false paradigm. Physicians (MDs and DOs) in our country practice a type of medicine called allopathic medicine. Other types of medicine exist as well, including naturopathic medicine, homeopathic medicine, traditional Chinese medicine, chiropractic medicine, and Ayurveda medicine.

Allopathic medicine was inspired by Sir Isaac Newton in the mid-17th century. There are five parts to its creed and it is based on the philosophy of reductionism:

1. The body operates like a machine.
2. That which cannot be measured does not exist.
3. The body cannot heal itself.

4. Illness is not cured. Symptoms are managed with medications and surgery.
5. The root cause of chronic illness is unknown.

I am an MD; I was trained in the allopathic method of practicing medicine. It is what is currently being taught in our medical schools today. I don't remember any of the faculty members or administrators at my medical school articulating these ideas verbally. But, in retrospect, I can assure you that they were implied.

Take a moment to think about what these precepts mean to you and your health.

1. The body is broken down into parts, and each part is dealt with separately. Very little credence is given to the fact that the parts of the body interact with one another and affect one another directly and indirectly. There is so much we have yet to learn about how the body works, how the mind and body interact, and how we age. This information will most likely not be retrieved from a reductionistic mindset; we need a new paradigm, a holistic one, to answer these more vexing issues.
2. Measurement is the "gold standard" for evidence-based medicine (science), but medical practice excludes such things as character, the soul, and even God. None of those can be measured scientifically, and yet they still exist. "My physician is a Christian," you

say. I cannot refute that, but there is no place for God or things related to the Spirit within the medical hierarchy. Those in leadership put no credence in the power of prayer or God's role in healing his children. If your physician is a Christian, it is of his own choosing and his faith operates to his and your benefit, but I'd bet you a nickel he or she didn't learn about God from his medical school faculty; it wasn't a part of his medical school curriculum. I wish this were not so!

3. The body heals itself all the time. Non-displaced fractures heal; all physicians do is set and immobilize the bone, and let Nature do what it does best. Cuts heal after they have been thoroughly cleansed and rinsed. Innumerable spontaneous remissions of cancers have been described. There is no room in the allopathic physician's world for miracles, and "healing" is rarely found in his lexicon.

4. "Symptoms are managed" means that there are no cures for any disease. ***Wrong again!*** Managed disease (not healthcare) is just another way for people to take advantage of the system, to enrich themselves. It doesn't improve access to healthcare, increase quality, or lower costs. New research is coming out every day which proves that metabolic syndrome, Type II diabetes, high blood pressure, and countless other disorders can be *cured*; not just treated indefinitely with medications. They can be *cured* once and for all. ***It starts with prevention***.

5. Chronic illnesses are usually caused by self-defeating habits (addictions, cigarette smoking, sedentary lifestyle, for example), nutritional deficiencies (insufficient quantities of vitamins, minerals, hormones), or toxic environmental exposures. Your doctor may believe that chronic disease is a result of genetics, a slow virus or aging, but that is only because:

    a. He/she doesn't have the time to look into your problem any deeper.
    b. He/she is unwilling to think or act contrary to the "wisdom" of the medical schools or State medical boards, and is unwilling to deviate from the current standard of medical care because of the sanctions or reprisals any deviation may bring.
    c. He/she may actually believe that there is no other known cause for your medical problem.

Many ripples arise from the reductionistic pebble which has been thrown into the medical pond. Appointment times have been reduced to ten minutes, you (the patient) are asked to present only one problem to the physician per visit, heavy emphasis is now placed on lab results and medical imaging procedures (ultrasound, CT, MRI, and so forth), and most of your questions are answered with a prescription for medication. Can you begin to see why Americans are profoundly unhealthy and longevity in this country has decreased over the past four years?

Transformation, Change, and A New Direction

Not only are the results of this brand of health delivery suboptimal, but patient satisfaction suffers, too. In fact, it is at an all-time low. Is everything being done that can be done to help each person? The answer is an emphatic *no!*

The type of medicine that is practiced in this country now is better-termed **sick-care, *not* healthcare**. Most of us are not coached or mentored about what to do to remain healthy, especially as we get older. We are taught how to suppress symptoms when they occur, and to gut-through an illness even though we are functioning suboptimally and exposing others to the same malady we have. We do not listen to our own bodies. Worse yet, we have abdicated responsibility for our own healthcare to others who do not always have our best interest at heart.

When was the last time a medical professional talked with you at length about preventing disease? Has anyone suggested to you that catching disease early, while it is manageable in scope and relatively easy to treat (maybe even curable), is preferable to neglecting your health until you develop a disease or condition which cannot be easily managed and eventually leads to your demise?

We have been conditioned to believe that "aging" is a natural part of life. It is miserable and inescapable. The "Golden Years" are just no fun, some say.

Well ... what if it was *not* normal to suffer aches and pains as we move past 50 years of age? What if we could remain vital and productive, without stiffness or frailty, well into our 90s and beyond? What if it was normal to live to 120 years of age without symptoms, enjoying our family and friends for many years, and enjoying our sunset years as much or more than our early years?

What if aging was actually a disease too, just like heart disease, cancer, diabetes, and Alzheimer's disease, and that it could be successfully managed or *even reversed* as we get older?

How would *that* make you feel?

Would you have a new spring in your step, and a new purpose for getting up every morning? I would!

I am here to tell you that there is **great news** coming soon about our healthcare — and it is not too far away!

I won't tease you or hold you in suspense much longer ... here is what I mean.

Let's lay the foundation for the monumental changes which lie ahead of us by looking for a moment at history. Most of the history of mankind has been local and linear. In the past, men and women, boys and girls, spent their short time on earth in one general area, and moved logically from

Transformation, Change, and A New Direction

one step to the next from birth through life to death. We wanted to control our lives as best we could; we craved certainty and predictability.

Technological breakthroughs moved us from one historical period to the next as a society, but occurred slowly enough to allow society to adapt with the change. Farming and metal tools ushered in the Agricultural Age from the Neolithic Age. The Scientific Age began in 1543 (when Galileo proved that the planets orbited the sun), and continued when Sir Isaac Newton published *Principia* in 1697, describing the laws of motion and gravity. This age of discovery was enhanced and accelerated when Gutenberg introduced his movable type printing press.

The Industrial Age began in the mid-18th Century, built around the steam engine (James Watt) and the cotton gin (Eli Whitney). The core of the Industrial Age was the generation and distribution of steam power, and ultimately electricity.

The fiber-optic cable and smaller, faster personal computers moved us into the Information Age (Digital Age) with gusto in the mid-20th Century. Unlike previous epochs in history, this Age allowed the gathering and generation of data, as well as storage and distribution of information at incredible speeds.

Rick Redd, MD

The World was connected together like never before, and had moved in a quantum leap from a linear, local, and logical (usually understandable) existence to a chaotic one, where there are aspects which cannot be seen, proven, or even imagined. This is the exponential world of the supralogical (translogical). Much about the world does not make sense yet, *and* it is moving so quickly that it is difficult to understand and to effectively apply the new rules which seem to govern it.

Let's see what we do know.

Why are these changes in medicine becoming evident now?

1. We have seen an exponential growth in computer power (supercomputers) to generate and organize large data bases from research facilities and data banks all over the world.
2. We can store massive amounts of data cheaply and retrieve this data at unprecedented speeds.
3. There has been a convergence of accelerating biotechnologies. Through artificial intelligence, computers were taught how to learn using algorithms and to make reasoned predictions about the environment. Amazon and Netflix use this technology to make suggestions for each of us every day. When combined with robotics or gene therapy, medical progress has been unmatched.

Transformation, Change, and A New Direction

4. Neural networks, constructed like the brain, are capable of unsupervised learning using chaotic data. These networks were used to successfully teach computers how to play chess, and in medicine to predict the function of proteins according to their 3D folding characteristics.
5. The information we need can be distributed at lightning speed throughout the country and the world because of a vast network of fiber-optic cable.
6. As computers get faster and faster, innovators and entrepreneurs have more time to discover new ideas which help mankind.
7. An abundance of capital (money) being invested in biotechnology companies means that more people can be hired. More equipment can also be bought, and more research can be done until breakthroughs are made.

How can this new technology be useful in medicine, and specifically aging? Because of the new technology, the medicine we are moving toward will be different and better. It will be more directed, more personalized, and more precise.

Here are three examples:

1. Artificial intelligence can be utilized to analyze each patient's DNA makeup. This makes it possible to determine which cancers might be likely in future

years. It will also help personalize diet and exercise so that both are matched with what makes us healthiest.
2. Pluripotent stem cells (retrieved from the placenta or cord blood) can be used to repopulate cartilage cells in joints where severe degenerative joint disease is present. This may make joint replacement obsolete. These cells have also been used in rotator cuff tears of the shoulder, obviating the need for surgery and extensive rehabilitation. This will save untold amounts of pain, recovery time, and money.

   Stem cells have also been used in palliating low back pain, as they can differentiate along whatever cell line that is needed in the body.

   Stem cells have also successfully been used in the treatment of blood cancers like lymphoma and leukemia.

   Placental and cord blood stem cells are very potent and not as likely to be contaminated with epigenetic factors, like viruses, pesticides, and heavy metals. Embryonic stem cells carry added unwanted ethical baggage because they originate from fetuses, and one cannot always be sure of the circumstances by which the cells were obtained. One could conceivably use autologous stem cells (from one's own bone marrow), but they are usually older cells with less potency.
3. A company called Bionaut Labs has designed remote-controlled microbots which can be injected into the vascular system and directed remotely with magnetic forces in order to deliver their payload (medications,

nutraceuticals, killer cells, or micro coils) within millimeters of the desired location. Why is this important? Therapies can be delivered *precisely* where they are needed. This differs from other therapies, such as chemotherapy and irradiation, where normal cells and abnormal cells are located within the treatment circle. Why injure normal cells, when it is the cancerous or inflammatory cells which you are trying to eliminate?

There are many other innovative medical ideas out there, designed specifically to aid you in being vital and productive throughout your life. Are you excited yet? **It is your turn; it is our turn.**

How do we, as patients, capitalize on these improvements? Some are ready for primetime now. I would refer you to Tony Robbins' new book *Life Force* for a list of the diagnostic tests and therapies which are available now. Other ideas have yet to be fully developed or FDA approved. Regardless, no matter when these ideas become tangible and usable, I would strongly urge the following:

1. <u>Take responsibility for your healthcare **today**</u>. Become a student of your body and of the innovative ways that disease can be defeated or slowed, and the ravages of time can be turned back. No one cares more about your healthcare than you do—no one! It is up to you to stay current and vigilant.

2. <u>Catch disease early when it is most treatable</u>. Get that yearly medical check-up. Be aggressive about treating what ails you in the safest and most efficacious way possible.
3. <u>Keep the ethics and morality of all diagnostic and treatment modalities in mind</u>. Do nothing to compromise your integrity. There is great potential for good, but an equal possibility for evil. Money, prestige and quest for power needs to be minimized to the extent that it can. Those who cannot play well with others in the "sandbox," need not be eligible to play at all. We must do the right things for the right reasons, and always keep God plugged into the equation.
4. <u>Do all that you can **now** to keep yourself alive and healthy so that you can take advantage of these innovative ideas when they become available</u>. My book, ***All-In or Nothing <u>Beyond</u> Retirement***, gives patients a holistic method for approaching healthcare, and a number of options for maintaining one's vitality and productivity as chronological age advances. Go to www.all-inornothing.com and order your autographed copy today.

We are on the cusp of life-changing innovations in medical care unlike we have ever seen before. With the new technological innovations, the availability of investment capital and a positive, moral, healthy mindset, we can sail into the next 50 years with incredible optimism and a well-founded belief that life will be better.

Transformation, Change, and A New Direction

Keep your powder dry, and your eye on the prize!
This is an exciting time to be alive!
God speed!

Notes:
1. Redd, Richard A. MD. ***All-in or Nothing Beyond Retirement***. Fort Worth: Creative Team Publishing, 2022.
2. Robbins, Tony, Peter Diamandis MD and Robert Hariri MD, PhD. ***Life Force***. New York: Simon & Schuster, 2022.
3. Information Age. Wikipedia.

From Rick:

How I met Glen Aubrey:

I was introduced to Glen in 2019 by a mutual friend, LTG Bob Dees. I had just retired from Radiology, and I felt like it was finally time to put some of my thoughts about "healthcare" and medicine on paper. I was looking for an experienced, Christian publisher with whom I could collaborate; I definitely needed a guide who could help me negotiate the bureaucratic morass of the publishing world, but more than that, I wanted someone with a creative mind and a "heart" for the Lord. Glen had both.

I wanted to write my books from a patient's perspective so the books would have meaning and practicality for the reader. Glen provided that, and because of him, I believe that all of the books are more relevant and useful. There is much more "wheat" and less "chaff."

In the past two years, Glen and I have released four books for publication. ***All-In or Nothing * Master Your Destiny*** is geared toward folks less than 30 years of age. ***All-In or Nothing Beyond Retirement*** was specifically written for those of us over 50 years of age. Both deal with healthcare from a holistic (whole-man) perspective, and both provide *options* for improvement, not mandates.

More than just a laundry list of things to do, I try to provide perspective and logical reasons for incorporating these ideas into your life. A Study Guide accompanies each book, which serves as a personalized GPS to guide the reader through the book.

I am grateful to Glen for his mentorship in helping me get these projects finished. He has been a great encouragement. I hope each work will be a benefit to many people for many years to come.

We are coming to a point in time as a culture where giant leaps forward are about to take place on many fronts, including medicine. Many of these improvements will enhance the quality of the lives we live (less pain, increased vitality and functionality), and some will actually extend our time we have to influence others on this earth (longevity will increase *and* we will feel well).

Join me in a commitment to stay healthy until these advancements are released. The future is not as far away as you think! All is in God's Hands; there are no accidents in life, *none*.

Your time has come!
Enjoy!
God speed!

~ Rick Redd, M.D.
2022

How Rick Redd, MD, and Glen Aubrey became acquainted:

Our acquaintance began in 2019 with the publication of the first of four books written by this gifted medical doctor. His first title was *All-In or Nothing * Master Your Destiny* and was published with a study guide. These two companion books were written for anyone under the age of 30.

His next two books were completed in the latter part of 2021, and published in 2022. In contrast, these two books were written for anyone over the age of 50. Again, a book and a study guide were released together. Title: *All-In or Nothing Beyond Retirement*.

Personally, I have greatly benefitted from the retired medical doctor's sage counsel and recommendations. You may greatly benefit as well.

See all of Rick Redd's books at www.all-inornothing.com.

It was also a unique honor to have Doctor Rick Redd represented in two additional Contributor books in advance of *Whatever Is True*. These two publications:

1. *God's Plan Unfolding * Strength and Renewal in Times of Crisis* www.godsplanunfolding.com
2. *God's Promises * Every One Fulfilled* www.godspromisesfulfilled.com

A sincere and dedicated appreciation to Doctor Redd for his immense contributions to my life, health, and now holistic health. I believe you will greatly benefit from his publications, available at www.creativeteampublishing.com.

~Glen Aubrey
2022

*****

Conclusion
Renewal: Return to Holistic Health

By Glen Aubrey

Perhaps the term, "**Holistic Health**" has taken on whole new meanings and a fresh dimension for you. Now we offer this invitation to you: you are warmly invited to "return" to Holistic Health.

Health in all areas of our experiences (hence "holistically"), is God's ultimate design for us, and has been so from the very beginning. We are invited to "return" to that first and unspoiled condition of love, health, and harmony in life. This side of heaven, holistic health can be God's gift to us, though not completed until eternity beckons. Through God's redemptive work, we are told we can be "born again," living in peace and harmony with our Lord.

We are talking about God's work of redemption. It is available as a free gift, presented to us not from or because of anything we merit; rather, through His grace alone.

When the act of creation was started, it was termed "new" because it was new in the most primordial sense. Nothing preceded it.

Now, the invitation is extended so you and I can be *new again*. This is what we term *re*-new-al.

In the book of Genesis, God's work of creation (including mankind) was fresh, holistically sound, without fault, struggle, or blemish, right from day one with God. The book of Genesis begins: "In the beginning, God created …" Oh, to have been there! Can you even imagine the awesomeness of God's newly fashioned world surrounding Adam and Eve? It's called "Paradise" for a reason.

Key fact: God's creation of a holistic environment was *prepared* for the creation of all human presence, in advance. The Triune God's activities occurred before anything or anyone else came to be. God's unique creation was primary; it was in perfect harmony with His design and will.

Permit me to venture this: that in the fullness of God's initial relationship with humans, nowhere was the term "holistic health" more prevalent: including physical health, and all the ways the Apostle Paul detailed for us in Philippians 4:8, including the contextual verses that frame this scripture.

Here is Paul's list in Philippians 4:8 again, as a memory refresher:

Whatever is <u>true</u>,

    Whatever is <u>noble</u>,

        Whatever is <u>right</u>,

            Whatever is <u>pure</u>,

                Whatever is <u>lovely</u>,

                    Whatever is <u>admirable</u>,

If anything is <u>excellent</u>

        Or <u>praiseworthy</u>,

                <u>Think about such things</u>.

The Power of Thought

"For as he thinks in his heart, so is he." This verse is from Proverbs 23:7, NKJV. The context of this passage deals with a man with "an evil eye" whose heart (core) is without good intent.

Nevertheless, the truth remains: thoughts carry weight; they are important, and give birth to what they mean when a person acts on them. They can be negative and destructive, positive and uplifting, or a mixture of the two.

Here is Good News: when we alter our thoughts and dwell upon the list of attributes from the Apostle Paul, our results are no longer negative; rather, holistically positive and sound.

A return to holistic health begins with a soulful prayer. Your prayer might be: "Create in me a clean heart, O God, and renew a right spirit within me." (From Psalm 51, KJV).

The "heart" refers to the center of you, your core self, and your spirit is your connection with God. When your desires to return to holistic health are expressed with humility and sincerity of heart, God will meet you "where you are" and restore holistic health to you. All can become beautiful in a renewal of this magnitude, according to God's will and in His timeline.

The Bible is a book of redemption of His creation. He can make you and I beautiful again, in His time.

I am reminded of this verse:

Ecclesiastes 3:11 (NIV):

He has made everything beautiful in its time. He has also set eternity in the human heart; yet no one can fathom what God has done from beginning to end.

Renewal: Return to Holistic Health

Is this journey worth it? Yes, I believe it is. This return is the most accurate, genuine description of "coming home" that we can experience. Home: you are always welcome there.

From Revelation 3:30 (NIV):

> Here I am! I stand at the door and knock. If anyone hears my voice and opens the door, I will come in and eat with that person, and they with me.

Imagine you are a guest at Jesus' dinner table, and He has prepared it especially for you!

During my formative years, my mom and dad had placed an art print on the wall. It was of a dining table prepared for the guests. It was His dinner and His invitation. This table can be set in your home, your heart.

The caption was: "Come, for all things are now ready."
~ See www.carpentertheologian.com for a copy of this print.
https://www.carpentertheologian.com/beyond-the-table-in-the-mist/

*****

Glen Aubrey

*****

The call is to **return**.
You can be **renewed**.
This is **redemption**.

*****

Resources

These resources are available to you and those about whom you care. They are effective. Please acquire and inquire:

1. A Bible containing the Old and New Testaments. We recommend these:
   a. English Standard Version (ESV)
   b. New International Version (NIV)
   c. New International Reader's Version (NIRV)
   d. Amplified Bible (AMP)
   e. Common English Bible (CEB)
   f. King James Version (KJV)
   g. New King James Version (NKJV)
   h. New American Standard Bible (NASB)
   i. New English Translation (NET)
   j. The Living Bible (TLB)
   k. Revised Standard Version (RSV)
   l. New Living Translation (NLT)
2. The Navigators Bible Study Assistance: https://www.navigators.org/about/contact-us/
3. Franklin Graham and the Billy Graham Evangelistic Organization www.billygraham.org

Appreciation

Personal family, close friends, and acquaintances have shared life, testimonies, time, and counsel on many more occasions than I can list here: indeed, innumerable.

In putting together ***Whatever Is True * Return to Holistic Health***, I wish to recognize the book's Contributors. From their life experiences and dedicated study, their writings have enriched the deep meanings of Philippians 4:8. In order of appearance, these Contributors are:

1. Everett (Bud) Hendrickson
2. John Culea
3. Pastor James Patton
4. Mickey Straub
5. Jim Robeson
6. Rick Redd, MD

In the counsel of many, great wisdom, perspective, and truth are found. I am blessed, along with you, to have benefitted in indescribable ways from what you have read. I hope you, our reader, have gleaned new knowledge and a fresh sense of who God is and His matchless love for you as you think about all these things.

Appreciation

As one Contributor often says, "Enjoy!" Another proclaims, "God Speed." Both of these best wishes originate from their hearts and souls to yours.

Let me hasten to add this:

> "And the peace of God, which transcends all understanding, will guard your hearts and your minds in Christ Jesus."

We are grateful for the peace of our Lord, God of the Universe.

*****

The Author

Glen Aubrey is an only son, a father of a girl and a boy now grown, and grandfather to five boys (from the daughter's side of the family) and three girls (from the son's side of the family).

He has been a professional musician since the 1970s, and in 2011 he won an Emmy ® for a video (TV) and audio commercial production. He is a pianist, composer (see www.glenaubrey.com), and arranger of some six thousand pieces of music, some 50 original songs published through The Nazarene Publishing House (Lillenas) along with thousands of published and unpublished music arrangements. He has conducted and produced multiple singing and performing groups, including choirs in and for churches, Christian Camps, and Conferences.

Mr. Aubrey has consulted nationally on building business core teams (see Chapter Nine, "Think About Such Things") and programming arts team production, featuring mentoring and duplication for churches and related non-profit organizations located in California, Colorado, Virginia, Arizona, Oregon, and Tennessee.

The Author

Glen says he has learned much and continues to learn daily to walk with Christ, one step and one day at a time.

He is fond of quoting the gospel song writer, Audrey Mieir, who composed: "To be used of God, To Sing, To Speak, To Pray. To be used of God to show someone the way. I long so much to feel the touch of His consuming fire; To be used of God is my desire." Mr. Aubrey heard her in person in the sixth grade and that song has been part of his memory and use since then.

This is Glen Aubrey's testimony of God's profound provision and miracle-working power: "God is real, He's alive, and is working in hearts and lives today." It is his hope that you will seek the Lord fully, with your whole heart and soul, and experience His peace which transcends (surpasses) all understanding."

May His blessing be yours now and forevermore.

*****

The Publisher and Printer

Multiple facets of Glen Aubrey's life and mission are represented by these entities:

- o **Creative Team Publishing**
  (CTP) www.creativeteampublishing.com) was formed in 2007.
- o **Creative Team Resources Group**
  (CTRG www.ctrg.com) began in the early 1980s and is the parent company.
- o **Creative Music Enterprises**
  (CME www.creativemusicenterprises.com), Glen's sole proprietorship, has been active in the music production and presentation world since 1977.
- o **Creative Ministry Teams**
  (CMT, www.creativeministryteams.com)
  is a 501 (c) 3 not-for-profit corporation and has functioned since the 1980s.

Publishing printed books, paperback and hardback, is at the heart of the business and ministry entities. Our printer is Lightning Source/Ingram with locations in the United States and other international locations as well.

It has been an honor to do business with them since 2014.

The Publisher and Printer

Contact information:

Lightning Source Inc. (US)
1246 Heil Quaker Blvd.
La Vergne, TN USA 37086
Email: inquiry@lightningsource.com
Voice: 1-800-509-4156

*****

www.ingramcontent.com/pod-product-compliance
Lightning Source LLC
Chambersburg PA
CBHW030230100526
44583CB00013BA/654